THE NEW AMERICAN NAVY

Drawn by Henry Reuterdahl

THE OREGON IN CHASE OF THE CRISTOBAL COLON DURING
THE BATTLE OF SANTIAGO

THE NEW
AMERICAN NAVY

BY

JOHN D. LONG

SECRETARY OF THE NAVY
1897–1902

*ILLUSTRATED WITH DRAWINGS BY HENRY
REUTERDAHL AND WITH PHOTOGRAPHS*

VOLUME II

NEW YORK
THE OUTLOOK COMPANY
1903

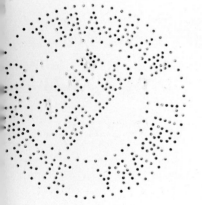

CONTENTS

IX

THE BATTLE OF SANTIAGO

X

SOME OF THE GALLANT DEEDS OF THE WAR WITH SPAIN

APPENDIX

LIST OF ILLUSTRATIONS

VOLUME II

MAP

THE NEW AMERICAN NAVY

IX

THE BATTLE OF SANTIAGO

By the mobilization of our entire armored strength at Santiago on June 1, 1898, the Navy Department made the natural tactical move which must have been anticipated by the naval strategists of Spain before Cervera left the Cape Verde Islands. We know that such was the expectation of the Spanish admiral and of his captains, though they considered either of the squadrons in which our fleet was divided sufficient to destroy their own. " Taking into account injuries and accidents to machinery, the necessity of renewing the coal supply, and other difficulties from which no ship is exempt," wrote Captain Concas y Palau, Cervera's chief of staff, " they formed only two squadrons instead of four, so that even if two or more of the most powerful ships were temporarily absent, the remaining

II

forces would still be such as to exclude any doubt as to the result. This is an admirable military precaution even in case of overwhelming superiority." So convinced was Admiral Cervera that destruction would be the inevitable consequence of departure from Santiago that, in response to a request from the captain-general of Cuba for an expression of opinion as to the plan that should be followed, he wrote: —

I, who am a man without ambitions, without mad passions, believe that whatever is most expedient should be done, and I state most emphatically that I shall *never* be the one to decree the horrible and useless hecatomb which will be the only possible result of the sortie from here by main force, for I should consider myself responsible before God and history for the lives sacrificed on the altar of vanity, and not in the true defense of the country.

It was the conviction in Washington, also, that an attempt by the Spanish division to escape would result in its annihilation. Yet there was the chance of one or more vessels running the blockade at night or during bad weather; and we were decidedly nervous as each day brought nearer the hurricane season, with the possibility of disaster as its accompaniment. It was difficult to get out of one's head the doggerel used by the sailor in describing weather conditions in the Caribbean Sea: —

June, too soon.
In July, stand by.
August, look out you must.
September, remember.
October, all over.

Sampson was as concerned about weather conditions as was the department. Before leaving
St. Nicholas Channel for Key West to obtain
permission to go to Santiago, he had sent instructions to Commodore Schley to sink the collier
Sterling across the narrow part of the entrance
of the Cuban harbor. This was not done before
the arrival of Sampson, though the Sterling had
reported on May 30, and Sampson at once prepared to carry out the plan. By his direction,
Naval Constructor Richmond Pearson Hobson
attached electric torpedoes to the hull of the
Merrimac, selected in place of the Sterling as the
obstruction for the harbor; sea-valves were cut,
cargo-ports opened, and anchor-chains holding
the anchors were ranged on deck, so that the
ship could be brought to a stop almost automatic-
ally. On the morning of June 3, with seven
men composing his crew, Hobson gallantly took
the collier into the harbor entrance, and, in spite
of the tremendous fire to which he was subjected,
coolly sunk her. Unfortunately an injury to her
steering-gear and the failure of some of the tor-

pedoes along her side to explode prevented the
Merrimac from sinking until much higher in the
channel than had been intended. Nevertheless,
the plan which was so promising in conception
was daringly executed, and Naval Constructor
Hobson and his men cannot be praised too highly
for the courage and patriotism which prompted
them to beg for and carry out orders which
seemed condemnation to death. Indeed, the
rivalry, not only among officers, but among the
men, for service on this forlorn hope, which
meant almost certain death, was very striking.
One man was taken from each ship, and in one
case, at least, a disappointed seaman offered his
accumulated wages for the chance of his successful shipmate.

The sinking of the Merrimac has been criticised; and yet, had it blocked the channel as intended, the Spanish fleet would have been ours
and have been added undestroyed to our navy.
Sampson quickly learned that the channel was still
open, and that the enemy could leave if disposed
to run the gauntlet before them. Our men-of-
war remained, therefore, as they had been before
the Merrimac was sunk, a wall against escape.
Coaling operations were at first conducted in
plain sight of the enemy; but Sampson recognized the need of a quiet harbor in which the

Drawn by Henry Reuterdahl

THE SINKING OF THE MERRIMAC

vessels could receive fuel without disturbance from wind and sea. Before he left Key West for Santiago, the department advised him that Captain Caspar F. Goodrich, commanding the St. Louis, who had been engaged in cable-cutting operations at Guantanamo, reported that bay weakly defended. Sampson was advised to seize it for use as a coaling-station, and he sent the Marblehead and the Yankee, on June 7, to occupy it. No fortifications were found, though the ships were fired upon by a few old guns mounted at Cayo Toro and a small gunboat. Even before this reconnaissance, Sampson had telegraphed to Commodore Remey directing him to prepare to send to Santiago the battalion of marines which was in camp at Key West. The battalion had been organized at New York during the month of April, and was composed of vigorous young men whose deeds were to show them also gallant and courageous. It consisted of twenty-three commissioned officers of the marine corps, one surgeon of the navy, and six hundred and twenty-three enlisted men, all under command of Lieutenant-Colonel R. W. Huntington, United States Marine Corps. The battalion was organized especially for service in Cuba, and the greatest care was taken to equip it for the arduous and trying work it would be

called upon to perform. The auxiliary cruiser
Panther, transformed into a marine transport,
sailed with the battalion for Cuba on June 7,
and reached Santiago three days later. She
was immediately ordered to Guantanamo, and at
two o'clock of June 10 the marines landed and
established a camp at what Cuban officers pro-
nounced to be the only position on the bay which
could be successfully occupied and defended by
a small force. The marines were not to hold
their ground without fighting for it. They were
attacked on June 11 by a superior force of
Spaniards, and were subjected to the enemy's
operations constantly during the three following
days. Protected by their valor, Guantanamo
afforded the North Atlantic fleet a safe harbor
in which to coal and make repairs. The marine
battalion, which was the first American force
to establish itself permanently on land in Cuba,
remained until August 5. It speaks well for
the equipment of the men and the vigilance and
care of those to whom their health and comfort
were confided, that not a single life was lost, and
only two per cent. were afflicted with disease.
Certainly this is a remarkable record, which has
never been approached by any foreign force operating in Cuba. It was a splendid exhibition of
brave and intelligent service.

Sampson lifted a heavy burden upon his shoulders when he assumed command at Santiago. He sank the Merrimac, occupied Guantanamo Bay for use as a coaling base, organized his command and assigned his vessels in the two squadrons into which he divided it. He prepared and promulgated plans for the naval battle that was sure to come, supervised the movements of the more than a hundred vessels within the range of his command, and was charged with the blockade of the whole Cuban coast, with coöperation with the army, and with the landing of its troops. His correspondence with the fleet and with the department was large and constant. No other naval officer had such an engrossing variety of duties. On the 2d of June, he issued his general order providing for the most thorough precautions to prevent Cervera's escape and for battling and destroying his fleet in case he attempted escape. Under it our fleet line was kept in an inclosing semicircle day and night before the harbor, closely vigilant. Every night the faithful search-light guarded against the enemy's escape or torpedo attack. Under the following clause of that order, " If the enemy tries to escape, the ships must close and engage as soon as possible, and endeavor to sink his vessels or force them to run ashore," the later famous battle of

July 3 was actually fought and the great victory won in accordance with the plan of the commander-in-chief, to whom is due the credit that is always given to the man on whom is the responsibility of the command and of the preparation of the plans for execution by those under him.

Meantime he had not lost sight of the importance of ascertaining whether all the Spanish fleet were at Santiago. On the morning of May 29, Commodore Schley had cabled to the department that he had recognized the Cristobal Colon and Infanta Maria Teresa and two torpedo-boat destroyers. On May 30, the commodore was asked to ascertain the whereabouts of the Almirante Oquendo and the Vizcaya, the remaining two armored cruisers, and on May 31, Sampson, when hastening to superintend operations, was told by the department that it was essential to know the exact location of all of the armored cruisers, as the military expedition against Santiago must necessarily wait for the information. On June 3, Sampson cabled that a reliable Cuban, acting under his instructions, had ascertained and reported the entire Spanish fleet in Santiago. " Beg troops move with all possible celerity," he added ; " of paramount importance." Sampson believed, and this belief the department

BATTLE-SHIP IOWA

Photograph by E. Muller

shared, that Cervera's capture or destruction would terminate the war. Major-General Miles, commanding the army, had expressed the opinion that it would be extremely hazardous and injudicious to put an army into Cuba during what is known as the " rainy " season, suggesting October as the proper month, and pointed out that another element of extreme danger would be the possibility of the navy being unable to keep the water between our territory and that island clear of hostile ships or fleets. Indeed, General Miles counseled that no troops should go to Cuba till our navy had destroyed the Spanish fleet. The War Department, more vigorous, determined early in May that an army under the command of Brigadier-General William R. Shafter should, with the coöperation of the navy, seize and hold Mariel, which was to be the base of operations against Havana. The appearance of Cervera's fleet caused the abandonment of this expedition. The arrival of the enemy's ships in Santiago, and the convergence upon that point of our men-of-war to blockade them, gave an opportunity for the army to coöperate with the navy in forcing an entrance into the harbor where it could destroy the Spanish fleet, and at the same time by an interior attack upon the city to compel its surrender. On May 27, the Secretary of War

was officially advised by the Navy Department
that on receipt of absolute information of the
presence of the Spanish fleet in Santiago " the
movement to Santiago should be made without
a moment's delay, day or night." Sampson was
simultaneously instructed to organize a convoy
for the thirty or more army transports, which
convoy should include the New York, Indiana,
and Oregon, and as many smaller vessels as could
be gathered to guard against possible attack.

The presence of the Spanish division in Santiago made that harbor the center of war. Almost
daily after his arrival Sampson cabled urgently
requesting expedition in the movement of the
army. He invited attention to the fact that if
there were delay the city would be defended
more strongly by guns taken from the ships, and
he asserted that with ten thousand men the city
and squadron could be captured or destroyed
within forty-eight hours. On June 1, a memorandum was submitted to the Secretary of War
stating that the battle-ship Indiana and a dozen
smaller vessels were ready to protect the army
en route to Santiago. This large force, under
command of Captain Henry C. Taylor, was assembled to deter by the mere fact of overwhelming superiority any enterprising Spanish commander from attempting a dash which might

cause disaster to the transport fleet. The army transport captains, who were civilians, were concerned more about the safety of their ships and the interests of their owners than about the necessities of the government. Never having engaged in such maneuvers, they were unable to maintain formation which would permit concentration of the convoy for their defense. In case of attack a panic might ensue, the consequences of which the department was unwilling to contemplate. It was therefore decided to organize a force the formidable character of which would forbid any plan on the part of the enemy to prevent the army from reaching Santiago. As a further precaution, Sampson was instructed to send a ship to San Juan, Porto Rico, to blockade the torpedo destroyer Terror in that harbor while the army was afloat.

Commodore Remey telegraphed on June 4 that the convoy was ready to sail. The army was slow in embarking, and it was not until June 8 that a part of it was prepared for departure. While those of the thirty or more transports which had their forces on board — five of them that day having sailed for the rendezvous down the bay and two others then hauling out — were moving out of Tampa, the department received a dispatch from Remey giving a circumstantial

account of the sighting off the northern coast of
Cuba by the auxiliary gunboat Eagle of three
Spanish men-of-war, one a protected cruiser and
the others torpedo-boat destroyers; and this was
subsequently confirmed by the Resolute. The
department could not understand this report.
Sampson had positively stated that the four
Spanish armored cruisers and two torpedo-boat
destroyers were locked up in the harbor of Santiago, and the only remaining torpedo-boat destroyer in the West Indies flying the Spanish flag
was at San Juan. The information was, however, of the most disturbing character. A request was immediately made of the War Department to delay the departure of the expedition,
and men-of-war were sent to reinforce the blockade and to scour the vicinity in which the enemy's
division had been sighted. The five transports
above referred to were ordered back. Remey
was asked for further particulars. He telegraphed that the captains of the Eagle and
Resolute based their reports upon personal observation, and that officers and crew of the former
vessel confirmed the statement of their commander. Sampson was advised of the discovery
of the enemy's vessels, and directed to send two
of his fastest armored vessels to search St.
Nicholas Channel and to reinforce the convoy

Photograph by E. Muller

BATTLE-SHIP INDIANA

which was to start immediately.   In the light of
information in his possession, necessarily more
ample and accurate than that of the department,
Sampson discredited the report, and cabled that
the vessels seen by the Eagle were the Armeria,
Scorpion, and Supply of our own fleet which had
been at the point where the supposed hostile
ships were sighted.   Sampson properly exercised
his discretion in not sending any armored ships
to Key West, reporting that even if the rumor
were found to be correct there was sufficient
force to furnish safe convoy.   In its message to
Sampson the department had asked him if he
were sure that all the Spanish cruisers were in
Santiago.   To place this point beyond all question, he instructed Commander Daniel Delehanty,
commanding the auxiliary gunboat Suwanee, to
get in communication with the insurgents and
obtain reliable information as to the character
and number of Spanish ships in the harbor.   Unwilling to trust the insurgents, Commander Delehanty detailed Lieutenant Victor Blue to pene-
trate to the shore of Santiago, and by personal
inspection ascertain the force that lay upon its
protected waters.   In the uniform of his rank
Lieutenant Blue landed, and upon his return on
June 13 reported that he had seen and located
all the ships of Admiral Cervera's command.

Decided relief followed the receipt of this information. Even before it reached Washington, however, and, in fact, prior to the inquiry to Sampson for confirmatory knowledge of the presence of the Spanish force at Santiago, Remey had been directed to reassemble and coal the convoy; troops were all the time embarking on board, and on the morning of June 12 it was reported ready for the service expected of it. It was not until 3 P. M. of June 14, however, that the transport fleet sailed from Tampa, soldiers continuing to pour upon the wharf and into the transports until the morning of that day, so that in fact the army suffered no delay.

To organize the convoy, it had been necessary to strip the blockade and coast defense force of men-of-war. For three weeks our blockade was hardly more than technically effective. Ostensibly to provide protection for Austrians in Cuba, the Vienna government sent the cruiser Maria Teresa on a visit to the ports of the island. The department was of opinion that the purpose was to determine whether the blockade was conducted in accordance with international law. This was also believed to be one of the objects of the presence in Cuban waters of the German cruiser Geier, which arrived at Cienfuegos on June 11, and which reported not a single vessel blockading that port. The commander of the Geier, in cruising on the north shore of the island, purposely " kept close to the shore, in order to inspect the harbor of Mariel and to see how far the American blockading-line extended." The Geier was somewhat inclined to neglect the customary amenities. On June 22 she was sighted off Havana by the Wilmington, to which she explained that she was from Jagua Bay bound to Havana. Commander C. C. Todd, commanding the American gunboat, signaled that the position of the senior officer was north of Havana, and he expected the German cruiser would communicate with that officer before proceeding on her course. But the Geier did not alter her direction, and shortly disappeared in a squall. She was not again seen by the Wilmington, having entered Havana.

Here were the men-of-war of two nations, both friendly to Spain, cruising in Cuban waters, apparently for the purpose of finding flaws in our blockade; and as their conduct was based necessarily on orders from their governments, the President could not but consider the possibility of the interference of the latter in the conflict. The advisability of guarding our armored ships by every possible means and of not permitting them to incur unjustifiable risk of injury by a

shot from a shore battery became more apparent.
The need of strengthening our blockade was also
plain, as indeed was the desirability of its exten-
sion. The department had learned that the Spaniards were receiving supplies from Jamaica,
Mexico, Europe, and North America, and it
feared that the demand for necessities would
cause the establishment of lines of steamers connecting neutral countries with Cuban ports which
were not mentioned in the President's proclamation of blockade but which were in communication with Havana. The main object of the
blockade was the reduction of Havana by the
peaceful though necessarily distressing expedient
of cutting off supplies. It was destined to failure unless the cordon about Cuba were extended.
The department therefore determined to recommend the blockade of the coast of Cuba from
Cape Francis near the Yucatan Channel, in Cape
Cruz, a short distance to the westward of Santiago. As the vessels carrying supplies to Havana usually entered Batabano which was in
railroad communication with the capital, that port
was necessarily included within the limits of the
blockade. A few miles from Batabano lies the
Isle of Pines. This it was determined to seize
for use as a base and harbor of refuge for small
vessels operating in its vicinity, and at the time

THE LATE REAR–ADMIRAL JOHN W. PHILIP

In command of the battle-ship Texas during the war

the peace protocol was signed the marine battalion which had done such excellent work at Guantanamo was on its way to effect occupation.

A further complication was added to the war situation when the State Department was advised on June 18 that the reserve fleet of Spain, consisting of one battle-ship, one armored cruiser, six converted cruisers, and four destroyers, besides auxiliary vessels, under the command of Admiral Camara, was on its way to the Philippines from the Spanish Peninsula. A week before the report of Camara's departure reached the Navy Department, the monitor Monterey sailed from San Diego, California, via Honolulu and Guam, and on June 23 the Monadnock left San Francisco for the same destination — both intended for reinforcement to Dewey. But the monitors were slow, and we could not count upon their arrival in advance of the Spanish fleet. It became necessary to employ other means to reinforce Dewey. Commodore John C. Watson was detached from the command of the blockading division on the north coast of Cuba and directed to hasten with dispatch to Santiago, where he was to assume command of a squadron consisting of the battle-ships Iowa and Oregon and the cruisers Newark, Yosemite, Yankee, and Dixie.

II

That the vessels might not suffer from want of fuel, a number of steam colliers, carrying forty thousand tons of the best coal of the country, were assembled at Hampton Roads, and instructions were given them to join Watson in the Azore Islands. Hitherto the department had attempted, with poor success, to keep news of its orders and plans from the press. On this occasion, however, the plan of a direct attack upon Spain was given the widest publicity, with a view primarily to alarm Spain and cause the recall of Camara, and secondarily to awaken Europe to the fact that the republic of the western hemisphere would not hesitate to carry war, if necessary, across the Atlantic. Announcement was made on June 27 of the organization of Commodore Watson's squadron, officially designated as the " Eastern Squadron," which "will sail for the coast of Spain immediately."

Departure of Camara's reserve fleet left the coast of Spain practically without naval defense, but public opinion and the desire to assert sovereignty in the Philippines forced the Madrid authorities to make the move. For a moment, Spain had considered the withdrawal of Cervera from Santiago, unaware that his return was impossible; but the captain-general of Cuba frowned on such action. The inadequacy of their home fortifications was known to the Castilians better than to us. But Watson's real destination was not a Spanish port. It was intended that he should follow Camara's fleet, and he would have experienced little difficulty, though reaching the East after its arrival there, in arranging a junction with Dewey. A combined movement by them against the enemy's forces would have insured their annihilation.

The Spanish reserve fleet arrived at Port Saïd on June 26, and the fact was cabled to Dewey. Sampson was also advised of the distance it had made, but he was loath to part with any of his ships because of his opinion that the force he then had " insures a capture which I believe will terminate the war." But the department could not leave Dewey with an inferior force. Our supremacy in the Pacific, with all that it meant, must be maintained; the troops en route to Manila must be protected. So, disregarding Sampson's views, it was decided not to change the plan with respect to Watson's squadron. The departure of the battle-ships was delayed, however, in order that the remaining armored vessels might fill their coal bunkers and maintain, for as long a time as possible without recoaling, their position off Santiago.

Our difficulty in making a wise distribution

of the armored vessels available was great; but the Spaniards, too, were having trouble. The Egyptian government prohibited transshipment of coal to the Spanish battle-ship Pelayo, and on June 30 Camara was directed to leave Egyptian ports at once. His failure to pass without delay through the Suez Canal cast a doubt upon his destination, or indicated that he was not properly equipped for the long voyage to the Philippines. Watson's departure was suspended. The first of the Spanish ships began passage through the canal on July 2, and others went through on July 5 and 6. In the mean time Cervera's squadron had been destroyed, and the defense of Spain compelled the return of the ships in the Red Sea.

Meantime not the slightest attempt was made by the Spanish gunboats lurking in the harbors of Cuba to prevent the American transports with the army on board from safely reaching their destination. The knowledge of the formidable character of the fleet convoying it was sufficient to deter even the boldest from making a dash upon it. Before the departure of the expedition, the plan of campaign to be pursued jointly by the army and navy upon arrival at Santiago had been fully discussed by the War and Navy departments. Major-General William R. Shafter, commanding the military force, was directed by Gen-

CAPTAIN FRENCH ENSOR CHADWICK

In command of the armored cruiser New York during the war

eral R. A. Alger, Secretary of War, to proceed
with his expedition " under convoy of the navy
to the vicinity of Santiago de Cuba, land your
force at such place east and west of that point as
your judgment may dictate, under the protection
of the navy, and move it on to high ground and
bluffs overlooking the harbor or into the interior,
as shall best enable you to capture or destroy the
garrison there; and cover the navy as it sends
its men in small boats to remove torpedoes, or,
with the aid of the navy, capture or destroy the
Spanish fleet now reported to be in Santiago
Harbor."

It was the confident expectation of the service
that the army would attack from the rear the
Spanish shore batteries which Sampson found no
difficulty in silencing. It was suggested to the
President by the Navy Department that the
important bridge of Juragua, reported mined and
guarded by a small force of Spanish soldiers,
should be seized and held by the army as an incident to such an attack. With it in the possession of the army a great advantage in a movement on the rear of the forts would be achieved.
As the fleet would be employed in raising the
mines and attacking the Spanish vessels within
the harbor, the department expressed the opinion
that no body of seamen were needed or should

be landed for participation in the attempt on the bridge. This memorandum to the President was transmitted by the Secretary of War to General Shafter.

On the day of the army's arrival, on the 21st of June, Captain French E. Chadwick, commanding the armored cruiser New York, and Sampson's chief of staff, was sent to confer with General Shafter. Captain Chadwick pointed out on a chart which he brought the positions occupied by the eastern and western batteries, the carrying of which was regarded by the admiral as of primal importance, to be done before attention was paid to the city. " The possession of these points," says Admiral Sampson in his official report, " insured the destruction of the mines by us, the entrance of the heavy ships in the harbor, and the assault on Cervera's squadron. To this General Shafter gave most cordial assent, and stated that he had no intention of attacking the city proper, that here (pointing to the entrance) was the key to the situation, and that when we had this we had all."

Following the conference of Captain Chadwick with General Shafter, the latter met Rear-Admiral Sampson and Generals Garcia and Rabi, of the insurgent forces, a short distance from Aserradero, and the plan of campaign was discussed.

General Shafter claims that he announced at this conference his purpose to move against the city of Santiago. In his official report, Rear-Admiral Sampson reported that at that time General Shafter repeated what he had stated to Captain Chadwick. "I do not know why a change of plan occurred," Rear-Admiral Sampson states, "unless it was that the troops on being landed advanced themselves so far on the roads toward Santiago before any specific plan of operations had been decided upon, that it was found inconvenient to divert them to the other points. I believe that such adherence would have resulted in a much quicker surrender of the Spanish troops, and with much less loss of life, excepting possibly to the navy, which would have borne the brunt of attack instead of the army."

By changing the plan and attacking Santiago, Shafter made the city his objective, when the motive of the expedition was the destruction of Cervera's command. From the moment of his arrival until the surrender of Santiago, Sampson believed, and in this opinion he was supported by his subordinates, that the capture of the fortifications defending the entrance to the harbor was the first and only proper military move, and once it was carried out, not only would Cervera's division be sunk or captured, but the city would fall.

As Shafter's position before Santiago increased in seriousness, his appeals to the navy to force the harbor of Santiago increased in earnestness. "Navy should go into harbor at any cost," he cabled to the War Department. "If they do, I believe they will take the city and all the troops that are there. If they do not, our country should be prepared for heavy losses among our troops." This cablegram was sent two days after the destruction of Cervera's squadron. The international situation, however, did not permit us to take the risk of throwing our armored vessels away on the mines in Santiago Harbor when there were no Spanish vessels to attack and destroy. We could not afford to lose one battle-ship; our efforts to purchase war-ships before the war showed that the acquisition of a single battle-ship was impossible. Moreover, as has already been stated, the attitude of Continental Europe forbade the reduction of our armored naval strength, because upon it we might have to rely for defense not only from the Spanish force in European waters but from an attack by the navy of another country. Sampson never entertained the slightest fear of the forts defending Santiago. "They cannot even prevent our entrance," he wrote to General Shafter the day before Cervera's fleet came out. "Our trouble from the

Photograph by Hollinger

REAR-ADMIRAL HENRY C. TAYLOR

In command of the battle-ship Indiana during the war

first has been that the channel to the harbor is well strewn with observation mines, which would certainly result in the sinking of one or more of our ships if we attempted to enter the harbor, and by the sinking of a ship the object of the attempt to enter the harbor would be defeated by the preventing of further progress on our part. It was my hope that an attack on your part of these shore batteries from the rear would leave us at liberty to drag the channel for torpedoes." Sampson finally determined to bring the marines from Guantanamo and with them himself capture the batteries, but before the plan could be put into execution additional troops arrived and the city surrendered.

It was gratifying to the department to find that it had at Santiago an officer who would not be turned from the course which was so clearly buoyed. The pressure upon Sampson to follow the procedure of Farragut was not greater than that applied in Washington. Sharp criticism was leveled at the department and at Sampson because of their refusal to risk the loss of any of our armorclads. Secretary Alger wrote on July 15, urging that orders be given the fleet to force its way into the bay. On the following day a cable was received from Rear-Admiral Sampson fully explaining the situation, and declaring that

" to throw my ships to certain destruction upon mine-fields would be suicidal folly."

The department needed not this explanation to understand Sampson's course. Before its receipt the determination had been reached to relieve him of criticism and to accept in Washington the responsibility for his refusal to enter Santiago, especially when, as stated by him, it was clear that the army could have reduced the forts from the rear. He was directed to confer with the commander of the army with a view to doing all that was reasonably possible to insure the surrender of the enemy. " I leave the matter to your discretion," the Secretary of the Navy cabled, " except that the United States armored vessels must not be risked."

The events described cover the period between the arrival of the military expedition at Santiago and a few days prior to the capitulation of the Spanish forces in the eastern end of Cuba. Before the departure of Shafter's expedition from Tampa, the attention of the War Department was called to the need of supplying General Shafter's command with means for landing at its destination. The navy was prepared, of course, to furnish all the assistance in its power, in the disembarkation of troops, stores, etc. The Secretary of War on the 31st of May advised the Secretary of the Navy in rather an emphatic reply to an inquiry from the latter that "the major-general commanding will land his own troops. All that is required of the navy is to convoy and protect with the guns of the convoy while the military forces are landed." Yet practically no preparations were made by Shafter to land his army, and this task fell upon the navy. How well it was accomplished is shown by the cordial acknowledgment of army officers. This satisfactory maneuver followed a feint on the west side of the harbor and the bombardment of Daiquiri, which was the point of landing, and of several other available sites of debarkation. There being a possibility that Cervera would take advantage of the opportunity to attempt to escape, Sampson reinforced the blockading squadron by the battle-ship Indiana, which had accompanied the army expedition from Tampa.

With that bravery and gallantry which have characterized the conduct of American troops in action, the army under Shafter pressed forward toward Santiago. Its advance forced Spain to come to a decision in regard to Cervera's fleet. Captain-General Blanco expressed the opinion on June 28 that the situation of the vessels in Santiago was the most dangerous of all, and that, if they should be destroyed without fighting, the moral effect would be terrible both in Spain and abroad. Cervera replied that, on account of lack of batteries to keep the hostile squadron at a distance, it remained constantly near the harbor entrance, illuminating it; and that this made a sortie, except by main force, impossible. " In my opinion," added the admiral, " the sortie will entail the certain loss of the squadron and the majority of its crews. I shall never take this step on my own account, but if your excellency so orders I shall carry it out." The position of the Spanish troops defending Santiago became daily more untenable, and on July 2 General Blanco cabled to Cervera that, in view of the exhausted and serious condition of Santiago, he should go out immediately.

Sunday, July 3, 1898, is a day which will live in the annals of the American navy. A fog rested over the bay of Santiago. It was the pall which was descending upon the power of Spain in the Indies. Outside, when the morning blushed, it disclosed the American ships gently rocking at their blockading positions, their bows in a semi-circle pointing each to the narrow orifice through which Cervera was preparing to dash. In bold relief, rising from the blue of the ocean, was the rugged shore, covered, save at the mouth of the harbor, with verdure. Sampson had arranged to

CAPTAIN FRANCIS AUGUSTUS COOK

In command of the Brooklyn during the war

confer with General Shafter at Siboney during
the morning, and at 8.55 A. M. he started for
the rendezvous, signaling as he left, "Disregard
movements commander-in-chief." This familiar
signal, as is well known in naval parlance, is not
a relinquishment or transfer of command, but a
notification to the vessels of the fleet that the
commander-in-chief is moving—in this case, out
of his usual place in the blockading line. The
blockading squadron was further weakened by
the absence of the Massachusetts, which, need-
ing coal, had left at four o'clock for Guantanamo.
Having taken a leading part in the pursuit of
Cervera and in keeping him in Santiago, it seems
a hard fate that she was deprived of participation
in the battle, and it was a source of especial regret to me that the Bay State was not among
those the namesakes of which did so nobly for
the honor of the flag.

The morning wore on with the monotonous
round of duties imposed upon the crews of war-
ships. These were at their day stations — farther out than at night. They were ranged in
the form of a semicircle, with the harbor as the
center, the Brooklyn holding the extreme left or
western end of the line, the Texas next toward
the east, the Iowa still farther east and south on
the curve, then the Oregon, and, as the line swept

in to the coast, the Indiana. Closer inshore, and not far from the Brooklyn and the Indiana respectively, lay the converted gunboats Vixen and Gloucester. The vigilance the ships had observed, the rivalry between them to be the first to sight the enemy, the danger that neglect might result in death or the destruction of some of the ships or, worse yet, the disgrace of the enemy's escape, caused constant scrutiny of the narrow channel leading into the harbor.

The fact that the enemy was coming out was discovered almost simultaneously on several ships. From a six-pounder of the Iowa, two sharp reports, the first to break the stillness of that peaceful Sabbath morning, reverberated among the green-covered hills. From her signal-mast fluttered "Enemy's ships coming out," but the breeze had not time to straighten the flags before there broke out from the Texas the same signal.

"We had just finished making the turn at Diamond Bank, amidst deathlike silence, everybody awed by the magnificent spectacle of the ships issuing from the Morro and Socapa," Captain Concas wrote. "It was a solemn moment, capable of making the calmest heart beat faster. From outside the conning-tower, which I did not want to enter, in order, if I should fall, to set an example to my defenseless crew, I asked leave of the admiral to open fire, and, that received, I gave the order. The bugle gave the signal for the commencement of the battle, an order which was repeated by those of the other batteries and followed by a murmur of approbation from all those poor sailors and marines who were anxious to fight; for they did not know that those war-like echoes were the signal which hurled their country at the feet of the victor, since they were to deprive Spain of the only power still of value to her, without which a million soldiers could be of no service; of the only power which would have weight in the treaty of peace; a power the destruction of which would place Spain at the mercy of her enemy — the old Spain of Europe, not Cuba alone, as many ignorant persons believed. The sound of my bugles was the last echo of those which history tells us were sounded at the capture of Granada. It was the signal that the history of four centuries of grandeur was at an end and that Spain was becoming a nation of the fourth class."

Most of the crews of the American ships were at Sunday inspection when the enemy's vessels were discovered. In the lead was the Infanta Maria Teresa, following her the Vizcaya, then the Colon, and finally the Oquendo. The two destroyers lagged behind, though the intention was that, under the protection of the larger ships, they should hug the shore and thus escape the fire of the American guns. To the lookouts on the American ships, the Teresa, as she slowly felt her way along the narrow, tortuous channel, looked like a small tugboat, but through their glasses they promptly identified her and the ships which followed in her wake as the enemy which they and their messmates had so long sought an opportunity to engage.

With an alacrity which bespoke gratification that the close of weary waiting and watching had come, officers and men sprang to their stations. As they ran, gunners and stokers stripped off their upper clothing. The moment was fraught with the risk of death, but it was filled with action, and the men who were the actors wanted nothing to impede rapid and accurate movement. Down in the bowels of the ships, the stokers, the firemen, and the engineers, deprived of the inspiration which the flash of the guns and the sight of the enemy give, feverishly threw coal into the furnaces, or sprayed the fuel and started the fans to put on forced draught, or watched the machinery and carried out there the orders which the brazen bell or the speaking-tube brought from their officers. Grimed with coal-dust, they knew that upon them depended to a large extent

Photograph by Habenicht

REAR-ADMIRAL CHARLES EDGAR CLARK

In command of the Oregon during the war

whether the enemy would escape. And who can describe the feelings of the men at the machinery, as they cursed the steam for its slowness in rising, and at the fact that motives of economy and the desire to remain as long as possible before Santiago without recoaling had caused so many of their captains to refrain from keeping up steam on all the boilers ? For only the Oregon was prepared for full speed — a condition due to Captain Charles E. Clark, the commander of that famous ship, and his chief engineer, Robert W. Milligan, who kept the furnace fires lighted — certainly a fortunate circumstance on that fortunate day.

" If the enemy tries to escape," Sampson had directed in the standing battle order of June 2, which had undergone no modification, " the ships must close and engage as soon as possible, and endeavor to sink his vessels or force them to run ashore in the channel." This was the command of the day. Toward the mouth of the harbor the American ships started. The Vixen, not to obstruct the fire of the Brooklyn, properly turned out to sea. The Gloucester, at the eastern point of the line, gathered steam waiting the appearance of the Spanish torpedo-boat destroyers, which Commander Wainwright, her commander, marked as his especial prey. And when the

II

Furor and Pluton appeared, he slipped the leash, and the Gloucester, herself a mere pleasure yacht without armor and with an inferior battery, sprang at them — David at Goliath — a lightly clad youth fighting armored gladiators. The example of the commander inspired the men. It was one of the most intrepid and brilliant heroisms in all naval history. Calmly and deliberately they aimed at the destroyers, the most dreaded vessels of the Spanish navy, and shell after shell struck the target. Upon the destroyers also our armor-clads turned their guns. The Pluton was soon disabled; she turned and labored toward the rocks upon which she struck. The Furor, a wreck, aimlessly maneuvered in circles. Practically broken in two by a large shell which pierced her midships, her bow shot up from the water, and she sank.

Before the tragedy of the destroyers began, that of the armored cruisers was in course of consummation. As the Teresa moved out of the harbor, upon her was concentrated the awful fire of four battle-ships and one armored cruiser. Captain Concas states in his book that the plan agreed upon before the ships came out contemplated the ramming of the Brooklyn by the Teresa; but if this were really the purpose, it was abandoned before attempt was made to put it into execution.

Captain Taylor, of the Indiana, observed that the Teresa showed no intention to ram the Brooklyn; so did Commander Wainwright. There were a few minutes when uncertainty prevailed as to what the Spanish ships would do. Would they separate, and, each pursuing a different direction, attempt to scatter the fire of the American squadron? But Cervera, whose flag flew from the masthead of the Teresa, quickly settled this point, and took a westward course, closely followed by the remainder of his command.

The New York and Brooklyn were the only American vessels credited with the speed the Spanish cruisers were reputed to possess. The distance away of the former vessel, therefore, made it even more imperative that the enemy should not be allowed to pass the blockading line. As the Brooklyn was rushing in, she repeated the signal of the Iowa, " Enemy's ships escaping," then gave " Clear ship for action," and a third signal, " Close up " — all in execution of Rear-Admiral Sampson's standing order. Signal that the enemy was escaping had been hoisted on the New York, which, though out of the line, was in plain sight of the Iowa, Indiana, and Gloucester, and not so far from the Indiana and Gloucester as the Brooklyn was from those vessels.

Thus the first move of the action was in exact
accordance with the instructions of the commander-in-chief. Their complete observance was,
however, prevented by the failure of the Brooklyn to hold the position which had been assigned
to her. As this cruiser was steaming in toward
the mouth of the harbor, Commodore Schley explained to Captain Cook, commanding the vessel
and a very brave and competent officer, that the
signal " Close up," meant that he was " to keep
somewhere about one thousand yards from the
enemy, so as to be outside of her broadside torpedo range " — although no such interpretation
was or could have been placed upon it by the
commander-in-chief. To this interpretation of
the commodore may possibly be ascribed Captain
Cook's direction to port the helm as the ship was
nearing the enemy — an order immediately confirmed by Schley — and the Brooklyn began to
turn away from the battle-line until her stern was
presented to the hostile cruisers. This maneuver
was executed while from the masthead of the vessel was flying the signal " Close up!" Having
gone to the southward a distance not fully established, but ranging between eight hundred and
two thousand yards, the Brooklyn turned and
ran parallel with the Spanish ships. Schley declared this maneuver the crucial and deciding

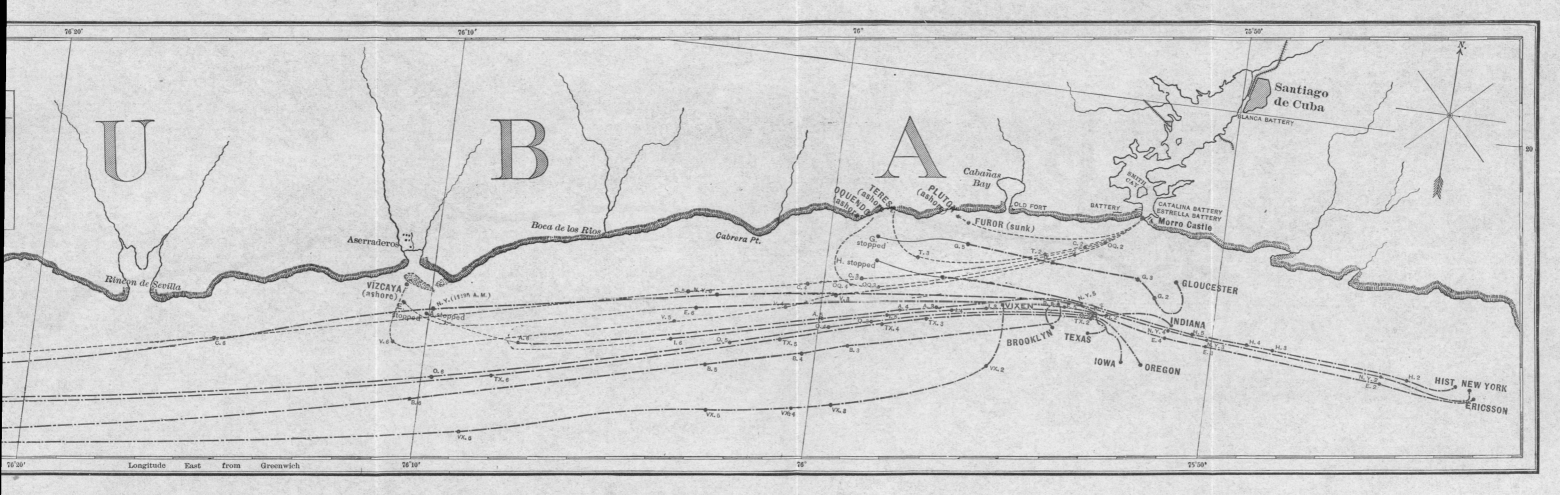

SHIPS OF ADMIRAL CERVERA'S SQUADRON AND THOSE OF THE UNITED STATES FLEET IN THE BATTLE OF JULY 3, 1898, OFF SANTIAGO DE CUBA

...tions of the different ships are shown by the use of the same numbers; i. e. when the Brooklyn was at the point marked B 3, the Oregon was at the point marked O 3, the Vizcaya at V 3, etc.

Photograph copyright 1898 by A. Loeffler

CONVERTED YACHT GLOUCESTER

feature of the combat, and that it removed him
from " dangerous proximity " to the enemy, — a
rather damaging claim which President Roosevelt
sharply criticised in his reply to Schley's appeal
from the Court of Inquiry. But it almost pre-
cipitated a collision with the Texas, which was
compelled to stop and lose distance in order to
escape the danger which was thus thrust upon
her, and it left a hole in the blockading line
through which the enemy promptly steamed.
Had the Spanish cruisers been able to make their
estimated speed, this disobedience of Admiral
Sampson's order to close and sink or force them
to run ashore in the channel might have resulted
in their escape. The Spaniards themselves expressed surprise that they were able to leave the
mouth of the harbor at all. " When the Oquendo
came out of the harbor," Captain Concas states,
"it is strange that the American battle-ships
which ought to have surrounded her did not capture or sink her then and there, because with the
superiority they had they ought to have accomplished more than they did." To those on the
Texas the moment of greatest danger in the
battle was when the Brooklyn loomed out of
the smoke. " Suddenly a whiff of breeze and a
lull in the firing lifted the pall," wrote Captain
Philip, of the Texas, "and there bearing toward us

and across our bows, turning on her port helm, with big waves curling over her bows and great clouds of black smoke pouring from her funnels, was the Brooklyn. She looked as big as half a dozen Great Easterns, and seemed so near that it took our breath away. 'Back both engines hard!' went down the tube to the astonished engineers, and in a twinkling the old ship was racing against herself. The collision which seemed imminent, even if it was not, was averted, and, as the big cruiser glided past, all of us on the bridge gave a sigh of relief. Had the Brooklyn struck us then, it would have probably been the end of the Texas and her half thousand men."

Once turned and straightened out on a course to the westward about 2400 yards from the parallel line of the Spanish ships, the Brooklyn did splendid and conspicuous work, lost the only man killed on our side, and did everything to redeem the error of her first maneuver.

In the mean time all the American vessels were covering the Spanish ships with a steel hail which smothered the men at the guns and prevented an accurate return. The Teresa could not stand up under the deadly fire to which she was subjected. Two twelve-inch shells from the Iowa or the Texas smashed in her armor and entered under the berth deck, exploding in the stern torpedo

manipulating room, cutting the beams of the berth
deck on the port side away from the frames and
completely wrecking everything in that compartment. A ragged hole four feet square on the
starboard side showed the point of exit. Three
eight-inch shells struck the ship, two of which
exploded, and the third passed through the hull
without bursting. Other projectiles also pene-
trated the vessel, killing and wounding men,
driving the gunners from their stations, and set-
ting the woodwork on fire. The Teresa was
soon a burning hulk, and at 10.15 A. M. she turned
to the shore and was beached six and one-half
miles from the Morro. As she struck the rock
the tars of the Texas, with the elation natural
to the victorious, began to cheer. But gazing
with pitying eye upon the sufferings of the men
lying wounded upon the decks of the cruiser
or frantically endeavoring to escape from the
flames which were licking up the masts, Captain
Philip, his heart bursting with the awfulness of
her disaster, cried to his crew: "Don't cheer,
boys: the poor devils are dying."

The murderous fire which had been poured
upon the Teresa as she made her exit from the
harbor was also suffered by the Vizcaya and
Oquendo. By the time the Oquendo appeared,
the gunners of the American fleet had recov-

ered from their first excitement, and they aimed at her as coolly as they had done a few days before at the batteries defending the entrance to the harbor. The precision with which they shot was shown by the effect on the target-ship. Her sides, smokestacks, ventilators, hatch-trunk, practically everything above the water line, were riddled by large shells or fragments and by numerous small projectiles. One eight-inch common shell struck the hood of the forward eleven-inch gun at the edge of the port and burst, its fragments killing every one in the turret and wrecking the gun and its mount. Six other eight-inch shells entered the ship, causing frightful damage. Like the Teresa, the Oquendo was soon on fire, which could not be extinguished, and she was beached half a mile to the westward of the point where the Teresa had sought a rest-ing-place. The Vizcaya and the Colon were now left to carry on the battle with the uninjured American ships. The Indiana, which had used her guns with destructive effect upon the Span-ish ships as they left the mouth of the harbor, was unable to keep up with the flying cruisers. She used her guns at long range upon the Viz-caya until Captain Taylor observed that vessel on fire and heading toward the shore.

By the loop of the Brooklyn the Texas had lost

Photograph by Parker

COMMANDER RICHARD WAINWRIGHT

In command of the Gloucester at the battle of Santiago

distance and position. Nevertheless she steamed gallantly after the chase, and, with the Oregon and the Iowa, drove shell into the enemy's vessels. The Iowa dropped behind, and Sampson, when he came up, signaled to her and to the Indiana to return to their blockading stations off the mouth of the harbor and prevent the approach of any man-of-war which might enterprisingly attempt to destroy the army transports lying not far away. This was the only strategic fleet order during the action.

Far out to sea the Brooklyn, which had been doing magnificent work with her battery after the loop was made, and the Oregon pressed on in chase of the Colon which was scudding along the shore after the destruction of the Teresa, Oquendo, and Vizcaya. Speeding to overtake the fleeing Spaniard also was the New York, which had now attained seventeen knots, the highest speed of any ship during the day. The Oregon, with a great white bone in her teeth, was overhauling the Colon, and, when within what was believed to be the range, a shell was fired from her forward thirteen-inch gun. The projectiles soon began to fall beyond and around the last of the Spanish cruisers. Further effort to escape would have resulted only in death to its officers and men. Following the examples of her sister ships in flames forty-five miles away, the Colon turned into the shore. The fight was ended.

We in Washington knew nothing of this dramatic struggle at the time it was occurring. The President and members of his cabinet sat discussing the distressing dispatch from Shafter saying that he contemplated withdrawal of his troops a distance of five miles, and considering the means to be employed for his immediate reinforcement. In the evening the Secretary of War received a dispatch from General Shafter transmitting a message from Captain Cotton, of the Harvard, announcing that Admiral Sampson had signaled that Cervera had escaped and that the admiral was in pursuit. Gathered at the White House on that Sabbath day, our hearts palpitated between hope and fear. Almost an hour later came a message stating that all the Spanish fleet, except one, were destroyed and burning on the beach. Then came Sampson's message: "The fleet under my command offers the nation as a Fourth of July present the whole of Cervera's fleet." Sampson has been criticised for this dispatch. He did not write it. It was written by the officer he sent to telegraph the news. But he assumed it, for he shirked no responsibility. The pronoun "I" is not in it. It is like General Sherman's telegram on the

capture of Savannah. It assumes no credit for
Sampson, but gives it all to the fleet under his
command. There is no fault to find with it.
Spain's power was destroyed. Santiago's fall
was certain. Peace was the inevitable and early
outcome. The destruction of the Spanish division released our entire battle fleet.

By the annihilation of Cervera's fleet, officers
and men had performed their duty. It was now
for the nation by practical act to show its appreciation of the stupendous victory — a victory
remarkable for the loss of but a single life and
the immaterial damage done our men-of-war.

As a partial recompense for their arduous and
dangerous work, and on the recommendation of
the Navy Department, Sampson was given by
the President, subject to confirmation by the
Senate, an advance in grade of eight numbers,
and Schley, six numbers; all the captains, with
the exception of Captain Clark of the Oregon,
who was given six numbers, were each advanced
five numbers, Wainright, who was only a lieutenant-commander, getting ten numbers, that advance in his grade corresponding to the smaller
numbers in the higher grade of captain. Advancement was given to the executive and engineer officers of the fleet. Save in the case of
Sampson and Schley, these promotions were

finally confirmed by the Senate. It is a tragic
feature of the struggle with Spain that Sampson,
broken by the tremendous strain he had undergone, died without receiving the recognition to
which his patriotic and splendid service entitled
him, and without even the thanks of Congress
or promotion in rank. And that, too, in spite
of the generous testimony of then Commodore
Schley, who, in his dispatch to the Navy Department of July 10, 1898, said: " Feel some morti-
fication that the newspaper accounts of July 6
have attributed victory on July 3 almost entirely
to me. Victory was secured by the force under
the command commander-in-chief North Atlantic Squadron, and to him the honor is due." In
a like spirit is the language of Sampson, the
commander-in-chief, in his letter to the department of July 10, in which, while compelled to
characterize as reprehensible (as the Court of
Inquiry afterwards were compelled to find it)
Schley's conduct in the previous May in his dil-
atory approach and vacillating retrograde off
Santiago, yet asked the department "to do him
ample justice" on the occasion of the battle of
July 3.

The unhappy controversy which afterwards
grew out of the rival claims of the friends of
these officers, and which came to be exceedingly

acrid, is the only incident of any moment that mars the otherwise universally applauded record of the navy during the Spanish War. Political and partisan interests fanned the flame of it. It raged more in the press and in public discussion even than in naval circles. Scurrilous verses and pictures in obloquy of Sampson were published, as if he had been a traitor instead of a patriot. The Navy Department, its head, and some of its bureau officers were bitterly assailed, and were without the slightest ground accused of persecuting Admiral Schley. In fact, the department had treated him with a leniency that with an earlier knowledge of the retrograde movement in May would have been inexcusable. It did not even order a court of inquiry until he, under the pressure of the circumstances, and after more than two years, asked for one. The considerate action of the department is fully set out in the Secretary's letter of July 3, 1899, to President McKinley in answer to the complaint of some gentlemen in Baltimore.[1]

Nor was there really any ground for this controversy. The facts were and are all of record and speak for themselves. With regard to the question of command at the battle of July 3 off Santiago, nothing could be simpler. Sampson

[1] See Appendix A for Secretary's letter.

was the commander-in-chief, as frankly stated
by Schley himself in his dispatch of July 10.
During the battle Sampson was at first at the
extreme east of the line, too far to take part then
in the fight, as the Spanish ships turned west
instead of east. But he at once steamed along
the whole line of battle, joining in the pursuit of
the last Spanish ships, though the fighting was
substantially over before he reached the Colon.
From the first he was all the time within signal
distance. The Gloucester was at the first less
than half the distance from the New York that
she was from the Brooklyn. The Indiana also
was then nearer to the New York than to the
Brooklyn. The battle was fought under and in
accordance with his standing order of June,
and during the whole day no order was given
to the fleet by anybody else in conflict with
that general order or in addition to it. He was
as much in command as Grant at Chattanooga
although Grant's generals were doing the actual
fighting at Lookout Mountain and Missionary
Ridge where he could not personally be. The
historian Rhodes comments on McClellan's customary absence from the actual battles fought by
his troops, and yet everybody recognizes that
McClellan was in command and responsible for
results, and to him is given the credit for the

victories and the blame for the defeats of his army. Sampson was likewise in actual and not merely in technical command. President Roosevelt in his summing up, on his rejection of Schley's appeal to him from the Court of Inquiry, says it was a " captains' fight." [1] This is true if only the actual fighting is referred to, just as, in that sense, it might have been said of Chattanooga. In that sense, as I said in an address at Atlanta, in December, 1898, the result would have been the same if both Sampson and Schley had been ten thousand miles away on the day of the Santiago fight. Neither of them was essential to the immediate battle or gave an order that day that affected the fleet's action until its close. It was, of course, fought under Sampson's general order in case the enemy came out, but that order had been standing a month and was familiar to every captain. As to Schley, as stated in the brief of Judge Advocate-General Captain Samuel C. Lemly and his able assistant, Mr. E. P. Hanna, the solicitor of the Navy Department and as substantially restated by President Roosevelt, not a ship in the fleet (except his own, the Brooklyn), neither the Gloucester, the Iowa, the Indiana, the Texas, nor the

---

[1] See Appendix B for President Roosevelt's memorandum rejecting Schley's appeal.

Oregon, had any order or command from Schley, so that, so far as any vessel except his own was concerned, " not the stroke of a propeller-blade, not the touch of a helm, not the firing of a shot, was done under the direction or by the order of Admiral Schley during that memorable battle." Had Admiral Schley not been on board the Brooklyn, Captain Cook would have fought the ship without a superior on board, as each other captain fought his.

It is not often that so bitter a controversy has arisen between the respective friends of two officers, where neither of them was an essential factor in the immediate fighting. On the other hand, in justice to them it should be remembered that Sampson, who was the actual commander-in-chief, subject to all the praise or blame that always attaches to the responsibility of that position, and under whom and whose orders the battle was fought, should have had his country's generous and ungrudging recognition, as Dewey had it for Manila; and also that Schley, although exercising command in no particular that day over the fleet, did his duty on board the Brooklyn (barring his turn from the enemy and endangering the Texas at the beginning), his ship thereafter rendering magnificent and most creditable service in its splendid fight with the enemy's ships and in compelling their surrender, and for this he should have full and unstinted credit.

History will certainly do justice to both men, giving them praise where deserved and blame where due. Would that the recent discussion of their merits, too often inflamed and unreasoningly blind to anything but its own preconceptions and prejudices, could have been inspired with the calm and generous spirit with which history at a later day and with judicial balance will record its verdict!

After the taking of the city of Santiago by the land forces and the gallant battles in which they engaged, attention was turned to Porto Rico. An ample naval convoy for the expedition to that island of the army contingent was provided by Admiral Sampson and even augmented at the over-apprehensive urgency of General Miles, commanding the army. The battle-ship Massachusetts was made flag-ship of a coöperating squadron. A division, Captain Charles H. Davis commanding, consisting of the Dixie, Annapolis, Gloucester, and Wasp, captured Ponce on July 28; three days later the Gloucester and Wasp took possession of Arroyo; the Amphitrite landed a detachment at Cape San Juan on August 6 and occupied the lighthouse, and the easy capture of the island was insured. Eleven United States men-of-war were in Porto Rican waters during the operations on the island of the army under General Miles, who — it is one of the humorous incidents of the war — sent an amusingly transparent telegram to the Secretary of War on August 9, stating that he was "informed the naval vessels at this place [Ponce] have been ordered round to San Juan. In order that there may be no conflict of authority, I request that no aggressive action be taken against that place, that no landings be made or communication held with the Spanish officials or forces on this island by the navy." I think that even the Secretary of War could not help smiling when he read me this unhappy dispatch. Three or four days later the war was over and there were no more battles or martial glory to win.

X

SOME OF THE GALLANT DEEDS OF THE WAR WITH SPAIN

BRAVERY is the rule rather than the exception. It has had signal illustrations in all the crises of our history. Who forgets Nathan Hale, who regretted, when dying the patriot's death, that he had but one life to give for his country?

When the war with Spain was impending, no question arose as to the bravery of American men-o'-war's men; nor, indeed, did we have any doubt of the courage of the foe. Spain's history is also replete with deeds of heroism. What the Spaniard lacked more than the American was the initiative dash which, supported by gallantry and efficiency, was sure to win the victory. Full of patriotism and from infancy inspired at hearth and school by the recital of the glorious deeds of the past, American seamen could be depended upon to do their best and to flinch from no service for the honor of the flag.

Associated in the popular heart with the names of our heroes in the recent war are the names of the vessels the decks of which they trod. It is Dewey and the Olympia, Clark and the Oregon, Hobson and the Merrimac.

At the time of the destruction of the Maine, the entire armored fleet of the Spanish government was in home ports or cruising in the Atlantic Ocean; and one vessel, the Vizcaya, was enjoying in New York harbor the hospitality of the United States. Because our force was not, at least nominally, superior to that of Spain, it was important that we should concentrate our armored ships within striking distance of Cuba. Dewey just at that time hardly seemed to need such vessels; his squadron was strong enough to destroy the Spanish force defending the Philippines. The geographical situation rendered our Pacific slope also safe from Spanish men-of-war operating from the Peninsula. Nevertheless, to guard against the contingency of attack by an isolated Spanish cruiser or privateer, a scheme of naval defense was adopted for the western coast which included the stationing of the monitor Monadnock at Port Angeles, Washington, for the defense of northern ports, and of the monitor Monterey at San Francisco and San Diego for the protection of southern cities, and the distribution of less effective vessels, manned by naval militiamen, at the same and other points. With these there, the Oregon could be spared from the Pacific coast and was needed in Cuban waters. She was in good trim to do the work the department cut out for her. At the naval station at Bremerton, Washington, she had been docked and cleaned and painted; to make her steadier in a seaway, new bilge-keels had been fitted; doubling-plates were put on; injured floor-plates were removed and replaced, and her outside plating was overhauled. She was in condition to render the best service, and her subsequent achievements in prolonged voyage and strenuous battle, and the comparative small cost of her subsequent repairs, are a splendid tribute to her builders, the Union Iron Works of San Francisco.

Three weeks after the Maine sank in Havana harbor the Secretary of the Navy ordered the Oregon to proceed from Bremerton to San Francisco, there to receive ammunition and await orders. " In view of the present critical condition of affairs," her commanding officer was advised under date of March 12, "the Oregon should leave San Francisco at the earliest possible date, and arrive at Callao [Peru] as soon as practicable. The crew is to be constantly drilled, the passage of the ship not to be delayed thereby." Broken health forced the department to order Captain Alexander H. McCormick, who then commanded her, before a board of medical survey, and its report of physical condemnation alone caused his detachment. There was no time, even had the department been so inclined, to send a captain from the East to join the Oregon, nor could one have been found better fitted for the perilous and gallant task before her than Captain Charles E. Clark, who then commanded the Monterey at San Diego, and who was transferred to the battle-ship. He entered upon his new duty on March 17, and two days later the Oregon began the trip which has no parallel in history.

The passage of the Oregon through the Golden Gate marked the beginning of a season of anxiety for the officers and men on board as well as for the department. Captain Clark was now to carry out the orders of the Secretary of the Navy, to proceed into a zone in which danger from the elements and the foe was to be feared. Primarily responsible for the voyage, the department was bound to facilitate it and by the transmission of information respecting the enemy to safeguard the ship. The Marietta, Commander Frederick M. Symonds commanding, which was at San José, Guatemala protecting American interests, was directed to sail at once for Panama, and under date of March 24 she left that Colombian port for Callao, to make arrangements for coaling the Oregon when the latter should arrive. The Marietta reached Callao on March 30, and contracted for coal. On the following day she sailed for Valparaiso, Chili. Her orders to put into this port were based upon the department's expectation that the Chilian battle-ship, the Captain Prat, would, by purchase, be added to our navy. The negotiations to this end fell through, as failed most of our efforts to buy men-of-war from foreign governments. The call of the Marietta was productive, however, of one important result. It afforded the Chilian authorities an opportunity to show to the United States the courtesies of their good will. On the day the Marietta reached Valparaiso the Oregon left Callao. While at the Peruvian port, minor repairs had been made to the machinery of the battle-ship, and she sailed with one boiler still in the hands of workmen. Captain Clark had cabled that he could make Montevideo, Uruguay, and perhaps Rio de Janeiro, Brazil, and the department gave him orders to this effect. He was advised that the Spanish torpedo-boat Temerario was at Montevideo, and that the Marietta had been directed to proceed to Sandy Point, Patagonia, to arrange for coal and to accompany him to Key West. Those who recall the apprehension excited by the Spanish torpedo-boats just prior to the war will understand the department's anxiety for the Oregon. There was the possibility that the commander of the Temerario might be sufficiently enterprising to take station in one of the numerous inlets of the Straits of Magellan, and discharge a torpedo at the American man-of-war as she passed. Captain Clark was not advised that war had been declared until his arrival, April 30, at Rio de Janeiro, but he took precautions against torpedo attacks, screening, when in company with the Marietta, all the lights except those shown by the leading vessel, and having gun-crews sleep beside the loaded 8-inch, 6-inch, and smaller rapid-fire guns. Nearing the Straits of Magellan, the Oregon and the Marietta, still separated, plunged through a tempestuous sea. Tons of water swept the deck of the battle-ship, and the little Marietta was tossed and pitched and finally compelled to run into Tuesday Bay. In the Straits, and before arrival at Sandy Point, the Oregon encountered a violent gale. So dense became the rain and the fog that it was impossible to distinguish the frowning shores. The situation of the Oregon was very dangerous. Captain Clark let go his anchors on a rocky shelf, and, with the wind howling and the waves thundering upon the

BATTLE-SHIP OREGON

islets and reefs, the gallant ship rode out the storm. At daylight, April 17, she got under way, and, steaming at fifteen and a half knots, hastened to Sandy Point. Captain Clark desired to reach his destination before nightfall so as to deprive the Temerario or any other hostile vessel of the additional advantage of darkness in making a torpedo attack. Tortuous and narrow, the Straits of Magellan afford numerous opportunities for the operations of a torpedo-boat.

The Marietta, which joined the Oregon at Sandy Point, had arranged for coal in advance of her arrival. The fuel was soon pouring in almost a continuous stream into the bunkers of the two ships. To enable earlier departure, men of the Oregon left their hammocks in the netting while they shoveled and carried coal. Equally zealous was the crew of the Marietta. The spirit on board the gunboat was also shown at Para, Brazil, where two officers, not on duty, seized wheelbarrows and voluntarily aided in coaling, thus encouraging the men, who, though nearly worn out by labor already performed, were full of enthusiasm.

It was impossible for the department to communicate telegraphically with the Oregon and Marietta at Sandy Point. After the voyage was completed we learned that the two ships safely passed out of the straits on the evening of April 21. The low rate of speed of the Marietta and the head winds and seas experienced north of Rio de la Plata retarded the Oregon during the voyage to Rio de Janeiro. The officers of the ship the engineers among whom voluntarily doubled their watches when high speed was required, and the men, who suffering from heat-exhaustion yet crawled back to the engine-rooms, chafed under this enforced delay. But the Marietta was needed to aid in repelling any possible torpedo attack, and man could not control the wind and the sea.

The department's concern for the Oregon was intensified by the departure of Cervera's squadron from Cape Verde Islands, and of the Temerario from Montevideo for Rio de Janeiro. There were indications that the Spanish ships were converging for the purpose of sinking our battle-ship. Many plans were considered by the Naval War Board and the department to assure the safety of the Oregon. Ignorant of the actual condition of the Spanish division, it was feared that if she fell in with it she would be overpowered. But confidence also prevailed that before destruction she would inflict serious damage upon her opponents. Captain Clark, in a letter to Captain Alfred T. Mahan, stated that in the event of battle he had determined to pursue the tactics of the last of the Horatii. He proposed to turn tail after sighting the enemy's fleet and to make a running fight. It would be to the advantage of the Oregon to delay as long as possible the employment of the broadside batteries of the hostile ships. Though three of the latter were sister ships, Captain Clark believed they had different rates of speed, and in a battle such as he projected they would be drawn out into a line, and one might be placed *hors du combat* before the others came to her assistance. By this move he hoped to prevent concentration of the Spanish fire, which, in all likelihood, would kill or drive our men from the rapid-firing guns, and leave the battle-ship dependent for defense upon her turret guns — a disadvantage which to an enterprising foe would be an opportunity for torpedo-boat attack. Against the heavy stern fire of the Oregon, consisting of two 13 and four 8 inch besides smaller guns, each Spanish cruiser could not oppose a bow fire of more than one 11 or 9.8 inch gun and guns of lesser caliber. Had the Oregon met Cervera's fleet, the latter, in view of its condition, would very likely have suffered defeat and perhaps annihilation. Certainly her

officers and men were determined to do and dare
any peril. *Possunt quia posse videntur.* The
tactics determined upon by Captain Clark were
observed at Santiago de Cuba, with this difference, that the Oregon, coöperating with the
other American men-of-war, was the pursuer
and the Spanish squadron was the chase.

The friendliness toward the United States of
Brazil, which sold to this country two men-of-
war under construction for her navy in England,
was further shown by the courtesies she extended
to the Oregon and the Marietta during their stay
at Rio de Janeiro. The department had been in
negotiation for the Nictheroy, an auxiliary cruiser
which during the revolution in Brazil of 1894
had been purchased by that government from a
private firm in the United States. The Nictheroy, as was the case with some other purchases
made by us in our sharp stress for ships, was
rather a bad bargain, but was at once overhauled
and is now, under the name of the Buffalo, a
useful and effective man-of-war. The purchase
served, however, the good purpose of increasing
the friendliness of Brazil, which had herself not
made an over good bargain in buying this vessel
five years before. Captain Clark was told that
the department left it to his discretion as to avoid-
ing the Spanish fleet and making his run to the

Photograph by Buffham

CAPTAIN ROBERT WILEY MILLIGAN

United States, and that the Marietta and Nictheroy were subject to his orders. Frequent breakdowns of the machinery of the Nictheroy delayed the division, and Captain Clark, feeling that the Oregon was needed to reinforce Rear-Admiral Sampson and that in any event he would have to abandon his consorts if he met the enemy, directed Commander Symonds to proceed with his own ship and the auxiliary cruiser to the United States. When the Oregon put into Bahia, the department instructed her commander to make no further stops at Brazilian ports, but to proceed to the West Indies, and reiterated its caution to avoid if possible the Spanish squadron, the whereabouts of which was still unknown.

On May 12, the day the department learned of the appearance of Cervera near Martinique, and two days after the departure of the Oregon from Bahia, the question of the safety of this battle-ship was submitted to and considered by the Naval War Board. The time for dispatching assistance had, however, passed. To send it, it would have been necessary for the department to advise Captain Clark at Bahia to pursue a certain route, and to designate a point on it at which he could be met by reinforcements. This action was not taken because, despite every

effort to maintain secrecy, it was probable that
information of the movement would leak out,
and, besides, the department was confident that
the Oregon would take care of herself. To the
Secretary the War Board reported: —

The board discussed fully the question of the advisability of dispatching assistance to the Oregon, in view of
the possibility of that vessel being waylaid by the Cape
de Verde squadron. After fully considering the matter,
it was concluded that, under conditions as they now exist,
it was inexpedient to detail either the Flying Squadron or
vessels from Admiral Sampson's fleet to assist her, as the
danger of her meeting the Spanish squadron was now
thought to be less than formerly, and it was undesirable
to disturb Admiral Sampson's operations around Porto
Rico or to leave the northern coast without its chief defense.

Sixty hours after the Spanish squadron left
Curaçao, its destination unknown, the Oregon
arrived at the Barbadoes, six hundred miles
away. Captain Clark learned here of the sighting of the Spanish fleet on May 12 off Martinique, one hundred miles distant. He coaled as
rapidly as possible, British neutrality permitting
him to receive sufficient fuel to reach an American port, and on the evening of May 18 he circled
the island and made to the northward on his way
to Key West. On May 24 the country and the
department learned with relief that the battle-

ship was off Jupiter Inlet, Florida, and a few hours later she dropped anchor at Key West. The Oregon had completed in sixty-eight days a voyage of fourteen thousand miles, and at its close needed only coal to join the fighting fleet. The Marietta, which had been authorized to leave the Nictheroy, and ordered to proceed alone to Hampton Roads, reached Key West on June 4. Like the Oregon, whose fame she shares, she was fit for immediate service — a remarkable record in view of the type of ship, the distance steamed, — twelve thousand miles, — and the character of the weather encountered. The congratulations sent by the department to the commanding officers of both vessels were heartfelt. The addition of the Oregon to Rear-Admiral Sampson's command gave it great superiority over Cervera and assured his destruction. The Spanish captains contend that the United States need not have felt a moment's concern about Captain Clark's ship. " It was about this time, namely, May 18," wrote Captain Concas y Palau, Cervera's chief of staff, " that the Oregon cast anchor at Barbadoes. The United States government was under the impression that it might be the object of the maneuvers of our squadron to go in search of that ship, which we, however, supposed to be in the Pacific. This illustrates how the commander-in-chief of our squadron was supplied with information."

It does not detract from the credit due and which has been universally given to the officers and the men of the Oregon to say that the voyages of the monitors from San Francisco to Manila were even more arduous and certainly as worthy of commendation. A vessel even of the Oregon class had never made a sea cruise such as she was called upon to make, and some were skeptical, before the battle-ship started, as to her ability to plough in safety through the seas raised by the storms of the southern zones. The department had, however, entertained no apprehension on this score, and performance settled all doubt. Then, too, the subsequent voyage of the Oregon from New York to Manila demonstrated beyond all question that she and her sister ships, under careful officers, can navigate the ocean without more than ordinary danger. The monitors, however, were nothing but coast defense ships, and had not been constructed for oversea operations. The experience of Rear-Admiral Sampson with the monitors attached to the North Atlantic Fleet had proved that vessels of this class are not good sea boats. Small coal supply restricted their range of operations. They

were slow, rolled heavily in a seaway, and were
almost suffocating between decks where officers
and men had to seek refuge even in a moderate
blow.

There was probability that Spain, taking advantage of the comparatively insignificant
strength of Admiral Dewey's squadron, might
order some of her armored ships, the completion
of which was hastened, to the East to reassert
her sovereignty over the Philippine Archipelago.
The official notes of Spain show that we were
not wrong in this assumption. " Very serious
situation in the Philippines," the Spanish Minister of War cabled to the governor-general of
Cuba, on June 3, " compels us to send there
ships and reinforcement of troops as early as
possible. To be able to cope with hostile squadron at Manila it will be indispensable to send
an equally strong fleet there."

Before this message was sent, the department,
through its agents in Spain, had heard and transmitted to Admiral Dewey, rumors of a possible
Spanish expedition to operate about the Philippine Islands, and on May 20 it advised him of
reports that the battle-ship Pelayo, armored
cruiser Carlos V., protected cruiser Alfonso
XII., and some transports carrying troops, were
en route to the Orient. Other reports gave the

east coast of the United States as their destination. Dewey was warned not to place too much credence in these rumors, as at the time our sources of intelligence in Spain were liable to error. If one, however, considers that the expedition under Admiral Camara, which started for the Philippines but was stopped at Suez, comprised both ships and troops, the rumors first mentioned will be found to have been very nearly correct.

The success of Dewey at Manila entailed upon the department the further responsibility of providing him with an adequate force to retain his position in the Far East. The reports of the dispatch of a Spanish relief force were regarded as having some foundation. For Spain to leave the United States in undisputed possession of the Philippines would be prejudicial to the Spanish cause in future peace negotiations. The cruiser Charleston, which had been hastily completed and commissioned, on May 5 was ordered to Manila in company with the City of Pekin, conveying troops to that point. En route, Captain Henry Glass, commanding, captured the island of Guam without resistance, the governor not having been informed of the declaration of war and at first believing that the guns fired by the Charleston were a salute to the flag of Spain.

Dewey had enough protected and unprotected cruisers and gunboats, but these in a battle with efficient armored ships would run great risk. With Cervera's squadron intact, and containing the possibilities of incalculable mischief, and with the probability that Spain would, after all, attach to it the armorclads then in Peninsular waters, any reduction of Sampson's strength would have been unwise, and was not seriously considered. But reinforcements for Dewey were essential, and the department decided to send to him the monitors Monterey and Monadnock.

There was historical precedent for the dispatch of the monitors on a long cruise. To silence critics who condemned the type because of alleged unseaworthiness, the department, after the Civil War, sent the Monadnock, of Civil War construction, from the Atlantic coast to San Francisco to be of aid in case of any necessity for the defense of the west coast, and the Miantonomoh to Europe to impress the governments of that continent with the formidable character of the new type of vessels developed in our country. Yet, in spite of the performance of these ships, the department could not but regard the voyage of the Monterey and the Monadnock to the Philippines, made under the very different circumstances of the stress of war, as an experiment. Again there entered the element of great risk, but the emergency justified it.

The Monterey was the first to leave San Francisco. Commanded by Commander E. H. C. Leutze, with officers and men enthusiastic at the prospect of active service, she started on June 7, in company with the collier Brutus. A moderate sea washed the coal from her deck, and she put into San Diego, whence she sailed on June 11. Two weeks later the Monadnock, Captain W. H. Whiting, troops on both sides of the Golden Gate wigwagging good-bye and good-luck messages, steamed for Honolulu. Accompanying her under instructions to supply coal or to tow was the collier Nero.

Thirteen days were occupied by the Monterey in making Honolulu. The Monadnock covered the distance in better time, arriving on July 3, ten days after leaving San Francisco. Both vessels made repairs and received supplies at the Hawaiian capital. On July 1 the Monterey started for Manila, and the Monadnock followed on July 13. The experience of one ship was the experience of both. Partly in tow, partly under their own steam, machinery requiring constant attention, the towing-bridle chafing, and repairs necessary, they labored toward Manila.

"The trip through the tropics," Captain

CAPTAIN EUGENE HENRY COZZENS LEUTZE

Whiting states in his official report, "was very trying on officers and men. The temperature of the sea water has been 85 to 87 degrees, the temperature of the air 75 to 95 degrees, and with the engines and boilers in use there was no chance for the heat to radiate. Hence the temperatures in the ship have been very high — fireroom from 110 degrees to 130 degrees, engineroom 118 to 140 degrees, dynamo-room 105 to 130 degrees, crew space, 86 to 99 degrees, lower wardroom 89 to 100 degrees, cabin stateroom 95 to 99 degrees. Men have been overcome in the coal-bunkers, fire-room, and evaporating-room with heat exhaustion, and the health of the ship's company has been affected by living in such high temperatures."

These hardships were common to both vessels, although little notice of them has been taken, and were much more prolonged and therefore severe than those on board of ships which had more glory. On the Monterey, and the same must have been substantially true of the Monadnock, the hatches were off only once in fifty days, and on that occasion the deck was so hot that it was necessary to play the hose on it to keep the pitch from boiling out. The monitor ran at times submerged under water. In spite, however, of all difficulties, no effort was left unmade to hasten the progress of the voyage. The Monterey chose to make Manila by San Bernardino Straits, and when she passed through in the early hours of August 2, the Spanish colors were hoisted in salute from a near-by lighthouse. The Spaniards apparently believed a relief force for themselves had come. At the time the Monadnock left San Francisco it was thought Camara might get his Spanish squadron to the East before her arrival. She was therefore directed to follow a prescribed course, along which she would join Dewey's squadron if it were compelled to withdraw temporarily from Manila. This course the Monadnock followed, but, of course, failed to sight any of Dewey's ships until she cast anchor in the harbor of Manila on August 16, four days after the signature of the peace protocol in Washington and three days after the fall of Manila. The Monterey had reached Manila on August 4. With the arrival of these two ships closed the most hazardous voyages of the war.

Thus, while all the ships fought well, a few were called upon to render conspicuous service, and they responded nobly. So it was with the men. There were everywhere in the service the desire and anxiety to be in the forefront, where danger was and where the flag needed support. It was pretty much an even level of courage, although above it rose some special instances of gallantry — special rather in the opportunities than in the men. There were, for instance, the deeds of Hobson, of Blue, of Wainwright, of Bernadou, of Ward and Buck, all of the navy, and of Newcomb of the revenue cutter service. Among the enlisted men were those who dared death with Hobson, who fought under Wainwright, who served with Bernadou, who bravely repulsed the Spaniards at Guantanamo, and who participated in the cable-cutting expeditions.

When Cervera's squadron was definitely located at Santiago, the department and Rear-Admiral Sampson considered the means that should be adopted to prevent its departure. The channel ranged from 350 to 450 feet in width at the entrance of the harbor, and it was decided to bottle up Cervera by sinking a vessel at the narrowest point. Sampson instructed Schley to use the collier Sterling to effect this purpose. Before Schley could execute the instructions, Sampson arrived and took command. While on his way to Santiago, this commander-in-chief directed Naval Constructor Richmond Pearson Hobson to devise a method for sinking a ship so as to prevent the egress of the Spanish men-of-war. Hobson considered many plans, including the feigning of a chase of a collier by the fleet with a view to deceiving the Spaniards until the obstruction had arrived at the point selected and had sunk. Sampson determined that it would be wiser to send in a ship just before dawn and when the tide was flood. This tide was desired so that if the anchor gear were destroyed the ship would drift and sink before it could be moved by the ebb tide to a wider part of the channel. Thursday, June 2, and half-past three in the morning were the day and hour selected for the maneuver. Immediately on arrival at Santiago steps were taken to carry the plan into execution. Ten electric torpedoes, each containing a charge of eighty-eight pounds of gunpowder, were attached to the port side of the collier Merrimac, which was designated for the sacrifice. To facilitate the sinking of the vessel it was arranged to drop anchors forward and aft, cargo ports and all interior doors and hatchways were opened, and sea connections prepared so as to be readily opened. Twenty-three hundred tons of coal lay in the hold of the Merrimac, but even if time had permitted its removal it was believed that it would aid in holding the vessel in the channel.

Rear-Admiral Sampson determined that as

Photograph by Hollinger

CAPTAIN RICHMOND PEARSON HOBSON

Hobson had prepared the plan, he was the person best fitted to execute it. Commodore J. M. Miller was therefore relieved of the command of the Merrimac — a hardship for that brave officer, but one which the chances of war imposed. A call for volunteers was made. Only six or seven men were needed — one to steer, one to assist in exploding the torpedoes, one at each anchor to cut the rope holding it, one in the boiler-room, and one to operate the engines. Rear-Admiral Sampson assured Hobson that there would be no difficulty in obtaining men. Indeed, when the signal was hoisted, the majority of the crew of every ship asked permission to go. Personal appeals were made to Hobson and to Sampson. Patriotism blunted the fear of shell and bullets, and glory-winning service of the country was the factor actuating the men who applied for the privilege of going to what appeared to be certain death. Sampson refused to permit a greater number on board the Merrimac than necessary for the conduct of the maneuver, and as finally designated they were: —

George Charette, gunner's mate, first class; Daniel Montague, chief master-at-arms; J. E. Murphy, coxswain; George F. Phillips, machinist, first class; Francis Kelly, water-tender; Randolph Clausen, coxswain, and Osborn Deignan, coxswain. Deignan, Phillips, and Kelly were among the crew of the collier when under Commander Miller. The commanding officer recommended Deignan to Hobson. Assistant Engineer Robert K. Crank, who aided in the preparations and was on the vessel on the first attempt to make the harbor entrance, urged the selection of Phillips and Kelly. Captain Robley D. Evans named Murphy as the representative of the Iowa. Charette had served with Hobson when the latter was a midshipman, and, remembering his conduct, the constructor allowed him to go. Montague was chief master-at-arms of the New York and was indorsed by the officers of the flagship. Clausen's selection at the last moment gave rise to the report that to make sure of going he had secreted himself on board the Merrimac, which was not the case. He was at her wheel when Hobson, in need of a seventh man, informed him to his delight that he should remain on the vessel.

Having completed arrangements early on the morning of June 2, the Merrimac, her crew stripped to underclothes, wearing life-jackets and carrying revolvers in belts around their waists, started for the scene of her destruction. Before out of reach she was directed by Rear-Admiral Sampson to return, as dawn was breaking. The reaction from the strain was fearful, and one man, Boatswain Mullen of the Merrimac, was, in spite of his earnest protest, relieved, and in his stead Murphy designated as above stated.

There was a slight chance of escape by Hobson and his companions, and Rear-Admiral Sampson directed the steam-launch of the New York, under Naval Cadet Joseph Wright Powell, to follow the collier and wait near the harbor entrance, prepared to dash in to the rescue should the men succeed in getting away alive. This duty was most hazardous, but, as in the case of the Merrimac, every member of the crew of the launch volunteered for it.

On the morning of June 3 the plan was put into execution. With the full moon streaming down upon the Merrimac, she moved toward the site of her grave. Deignan was at the wheel, Phillips and Kelly were in the engine and boiler rooms, and Charette, Clausen, Montague and Murphy were at their stations. Coolly directing the course of the ship was Hobson, stripped, like his men, of all clothing save shirt and drawers and wearing a life-preserver and revolver-belt. Five hundred yards from the mouth of the harbor the Spanish batteries opened fire, and shell hurtled through the air, shrieking and exploding in and about the ship. Hobson gave the signal to stop just before reaching the point where the Merrimac was to be sunk, and the men below obeyed the order. Sea-valves were opened, anchors let go, and orders given to explode the torpedoes. But the enemy's fire had broken the torpedo connections and shattered the electric generating cells, and but two torpedoes were discharged. In the mean time the steering-gear was shot away, and the wreck drifted helplessly away from the position where it had been intended it should sink.

The Merrimac was subjected to the fire of all the guns of the fortifications, and a submarine mine exploded beneath her hull. The Spaniards believed that our fleet was attempting to force the harbor. Lying at full length upon the deck, Hobson and his men waited for a projectile to explode among them and send all into eternity. The ship was drifting toward the wider section of the channel, and here she lurched heavily and sank. The men were washed miraculously alive into the water, and hurled about in the mass of débris. Toward a catamaran they swam, and to it they clung, keeping only their heads above the water. A Spanish launch appearing, Hobson called, and, covered by the rifles of her guard, he and his men were taken in. Admiral Cervera was on board; to him the Merrimac's crew surrendered, and his humanity and kindness were as great as their heroism, which appealed at once to his admiration.

Hobson gallantly executed the mission intrusted to him. Although it failed, failure in no wise detracted from the magnificent courage displayed by the men engaged in the maneuver. In his report of it to the department, Sampson said, " A more brave and daring thing has not been done since Cushing blew up the Albemarle." Learning with gratitude that the crew of the Merrimac survived, negotiations were begun to effect an exchange, and they resulted successfully a few days before the capitulation of Santiago.

While Sampson was satisfied on June 3 that he was blockading the entire Spanish squadron in Santiago, the report from the Eagle and the Resolute that they had sighted four powerful hostile vessels, although not much weight was attached to it, made necessary positive knowledge as to whether all Cervera's armored ships were actually within the Cuban harbor. Rear-Admiral Sampson was notified of the department's anxiety in this connection, and he directed Lieutenant-Commander Daniel Delehanty, commanding the United States Steamship Suwanee, to ascertain through the insurgents how many Spanish ships lay in the bay. Believing that an officer could obtain more satisfactory information than a Cuban, Lieutenant-Commander Delehanty, with Sampson's approval, directed Lieutenant Victor Blue to make a reconnaissance of the harbor. Clad in the uniform of his rank, Blue landed and, in company with a Cuban officer, made for the hills in the rear of Santiago. The two officers passed on one occasion within six hundred yards of a Spanish camp without detection. Blue was taken to the headquarters of an insurgent Cuban battalion, and there a conference was held as to the route to be followed. Small parties of Spaniards were patrolling the country in all directions within a zone of fifteen miles from the city, and it was necessary to exercise the utmost caution. A decision was finally reached, and, with three soldiers leading the way, Blue and the Cuban officer resumed the journey. The party traveled along the main road leading to Santiago for a distance of a mile and a half, when they entered the woods. Leading their mules through a swampy jungle and sinking knee-deep in mud, they doggedly tramped. Fearing that in the dark, night having fallen, a Spanish detachment might be met, it was decided

Photograph by Buffham

LIEUTENANT VICTOR BLUE

to halt, and until daylight they remained sheltered in the home of a Cuban sympathizer. When morning came, they moved along the road recommended by the host of the night. Other sympathizers gave good advice as to the route to be pursued in order to avoid Spaniards. The party finally reached the top of a hill and dismounted. Beneath it was encamped a force of Spanish soldiers, and beyond, upon the bay, lay two armored cruisers and two destroyers. The scouts gently stole toward the city, and half a mile from the first position ascended another hill. Here was sighted the third armored cruiser. But the fourth remained to be located. Another point of vantage was sought, and from it Lieutenant Blue ·beheld the sought-for vessel.

Having obtained the information, the party started on its return journey, and arrived without molestation at Acerraderos. The Suwanee's mail-boat carried Blue to his ship, and Rear-Admiral Sampson notified the department of the result of the reconnaissance.

Accurate information is, of course, essential to the successful conduct of war. Prior to and in the early stages of the struggle with Spain, the department received from various sources a mass of reports regarding the disposition and

condition of the Spanish ships. There was danger that hired spies would sell themselves to the
Spanish government and supply us with misleading information. The President and the Secretary
of the Navy determined to send two officers to
Europe to report upon the movements of Cervera and those of Camara. To the first duty was
assigned Ensign Henry Herbert Ward and to
the latter Ensign William Henry Buck. Each,
in civilian garb, was on board a foreign yacht
hired for the purpose, the officers and men of
which had no knowledge of the business or
character of their voyaging sightseer, except
that they were to take him wherever his pleasure inclined him to go. As these officers took
their lives in their hands, necessarily the greatest secrecy in regard to their mission was imposed. Ward first went to Cadiz, Spain, where
he stayed forty-eight hours but failed to find any
trace of Cervera or of the vessels of his division, though he identified the ships of Camara's
squadron and, safely reaching Gibraltar, cabled
the information to Washington. This information was confirmatorily valuable, for only the day
before its receipt the department had notified
Dewey that the Spanish fleet was en route to the
Philippines. From Gibraltar Ward went to St.
Thomas. At the Madeiras he learned that the

Canary Islands were defended by only three torpedo-boats, and this information was immediately
sent to the department. Spanish agents at St.
Thomas became suspicious of the young " Eng-
lishman," Ward and Buck being regarded as of
that nationality, and upon Ward's departure for
San Juan they cabled the fact of his coming to
the Spanish authorities. Four officials of the port
boarded the steamer when she reached San Juan
and cross-questioned the suspected passenger.
Displaying remarkable sang-froid, Ward was
guarded in his replies and finally declared that
he would not respond further unless in the presence of the British consul. The examination
was resumed when the British official boarded
the steamer. So convincing was the American
officer that he was finally advised that he would
not be molested, but he was not to be permitted
ashore. Not content with his narrow escape, and
desiring information in addition to that which
he could get in the harbor, Ward protested to
the British consul at being confined to the ship,
and through the intercession of that officer, who
little knew whose cause he was advocating, the
prohibition to land was removed. In company
with the consul and a Spanish naval officer he
landed and called upon the naval commandant,
of whom he requested relief from the espionage

of the Spaniards. This request was granted, and Ward strolled along the water front and through a portion of the Spanish barracks. After his visit to San Juan he visited neutral ports investigating rumors that the Spaniards were gathering supplies in preparation for further operations. These were found to be groundless.

In the mean time Buck was devoting his attention to Camara. Learning positively that the Spanish admiral had sailed from Cadiz on an easterly course, Buck proceeded to Port Saïd, where he ascertained that the Spanish ships had passed through the canal. Informed that Camara would probably return, Buck remained at Port Saïd, and when the hostile ships reëntered the Mediterranean he promptly cabled the news to the department. The departure of Camara from Port Saïd and his course were also communicated to Washington, and Buck then took passage in a steamer for Algiers, keeping in sight of the Spanish ships until the vessel he had boarded turned into its port of destination. From Algiers Buck returned to the United States, there being no further need of his presence in the Mediterranean.

Whoever tells the story of the battle of Santiago must refer to the gallantry of the officers

and men of the Gloucester. This pleasure
yacht, comparatively frail as a lady's fan, purchased from J. Pierpont Morgan and put to the
perils of a man-of-war, braved for a time, almost
alone, the guns of the whole Spanish squadron
and the shore batteries, and by her accurate and
deadly fire disabled and, with the assistance of
our armorclads, sank two Spanish torpedo-boat
destroyers, each of which was her superior in
construction and fighting strength. A successful
shot from a one-pounder gun would have rendered the Gloucester helpless, but, while aware
of this possibility yet giving no heed to it, Lieutenant-Commander Richard Wainwright carried
the vessel to the point where she could inflict the
greatest damage upon her foes. At the hour
when Cervera's ships appeared, the men of the
Gloucester, as well as of other vessels of the
squadron, were drawn up for Sunday inspection.
While on the berth-deck, Wainwright heard the
welcome news that the Spaniards were coming
out. Hastening to the bridge, he ordered the
helm put over, and to Chief Engineer George
W. McElroy the signal was given by Lieutenant
Harry McL. Huse, executive of the vessel,
" Full steam ahead."

The praise that is due Milligan, of the Oregon,
for keeping his engines in efficient condition is

due also to McElroy for his work in connection
with the machinery of the Gloucester. Wainwright ordered forced draught, and the blowers
were soon whirring, and steam began to rise in
the boilers of the gunboat. Her guns vomiting
projectiles, the Infanta Maria Teresa turned to
the west, and after her came the remaining Spanish armored cruisers. Almost irresistible was
the temptation to participate in the combat with
the armored cruisers, but Wainwright conceived
it to be his duty to wait for the destroyers, and,
with a patience difficult to exercise while part of
the quarry was at hand and shells were splash-
ing and raining about his little boat, he remained
near the Indiana. Suddenly from the mouth of
the harbor shot the Pluton and Furor, the dreaded
vipers of the Spanish squadron. " Gunboats
close in," signaled Captain Taylor, of the Indiana. Simultaneously with the hoisting of this
signal, the Gloucester, under full head of steam,
dashed toward the enemy. Bombardment of the
coasts had developed splendid gunners among
her officers and men. While waiting for the
destroyers, Lieutenant Thomas C. Wood, commanding the after division, made up of three
three-pounders, had deliberately discharged a
few shells at the armored cruisers, but the distance was too great for rapid fire. Closing in

on the destroyers, however, all the guns of the
Gloucester that could bear were brought into
action. Nearer and nearer together approached
these game little fighters — on one side orderly
procedure, coolness and precision, on the other
confusion, uncontrollable excitement and death.
About the time the Teresa and Oquendo sought
refuge upon the beach, the Pluton slowed down;
a few minutes later she was upon the rocks.
Wainwright now concentrated his fire, which
had been divided between the two destroyers,
upon the Furor which had turned toward the
Gloucester. For a moment it seemed that the
Spaniard intended to come to closer quarters with
her doughty antagonist. But the Furor was too
badly damaged for offense. She turned in a circle, and, seeing her condition, Wainwright sent,
to rescue any of her survivors, two of his officers, Lieutenants Wood and George H. Norman,
who had materially assisted in giving her her
deathblow. Some ten or twelve men were removed from the carnage and wreck, but before
any effort could be made to save the ship, she
sank slowly by the stern, an explosion occurred,
her bow shot out of the water, and she went
down. Assistant Engineer André M. Proctor,
who served as Wainwright's aide, was sent to
the Pluton, and rescued some of her men not

killed by the fire suffered by that ship. Without waiting to pick up all his boats, Wainwright steamed around a near-by point, over which smoke was rising. Here he found the Teresa and Oquendo aground. He resumed his merciful work of rescue, Acting Ensign John Edson and Lieutenant Norman in charge of the boats. Facing death through the explosion of magazines and shell, the men engaged in relief pluckily moved in the danger zone. Seamen Braun and Keller, of Ensign Edson's boat, swam through the heavy surf with a line from the Teresa, which they secured ashore, and under this line the cutter was hauled, carrying eight or ten Spaniards on each trip. Four hundred and eight men, a number of whom were wounded, were saved in this way, among them Admiral Cervera, his chief of staff, and other officers. Lieutenant Wood was also engaged in equally praiseworthy work, rescuing survivors of the Oquendo. The very apt and telling sentiment applied to the men of the Iowa by Captain Evans in his official report is equally true of the men of the Gloucester and other American vessels engaged on July 3. "So long as the enemy showed his flag," Captain Evans stated, "they fought like American seamen; but when the flag came down, they were as gentle and tender as American women."

Photograph by I. Villareal

ENSIGN WORTH BAGLEY

The daring of American sailors was exemplified in the action of Cardenas on May 11, 1898. Commander J. F. Merry, commanding the Machias, had learned that there were three small gunboats in this harbor, and when the Wilmington, Commander C. C. Todd, and the Winslow, Lieutenant J. B. Bernadou, arrived off Cardenas, he unfolded a plan of attack. Accompanied by the Winslow and the Hudson, the latter a revenue cutter commanded by Lieutenant Frank H. Newcomb, the Wilmington steamed into the bay. Shoal water prevented the Wilmington from approaching nearer to the wharves than two thousand yards, and from this distance it was impossible to distinguish the hostile gunboats. The Winslow was directed to steam farther in, in order to locate the enemy's ships. The Hudson, not better protected than the torpedo-boat, followed. When twelve hundred yards from the wharves, the Winslow received the fire of a gunboat and the shore battery. The Spaniards displayed remarkable accuracy of aim. " The Winslow at once began firing," Lieutenant Bernadou stated in his report, " and maintained fire until the end of the action with these ships. She was soon riddled, the steering-engine and forward · boiler disabled; one compartment set on fire." Though wounded in the thigh at the commencement of the engagement, Bernadou retained command. Steam and hand steering-gear destroyed, it was impossible to guide the vessel, but, with one engine still uninjured, Bernadou tried to zigzag his ship out of range. He gained about three hundred yards in this way. Signal was made to the Hudson for assistance, and the revenue cutter gallantly approached. With shells whistling and exploding about her, she caught a line from the torpedo-boat and towed her out of the harbor. Ensign Worth Bagley, of the Winslow, was killed, and two men were mortally wounded by a shell. These were the first casualties in Cuban waters. Bagley was a fine young North Carolinian, and for him and the brave men who died with him the whole country was at once full of pride and of mourning.

At Manzanillo, also, American officers and men displayed noteworthy conduct. Four Spanish gunboats were reported within the harbor, and on June 29 Rear-Admiral Sampson directed Lieutenant Lucien Young, commanding the Hist, to proceed off that port to attack the enemy's ships. Like the Gloucester, the Hist was a small yacht without protection of any kind, having a battery of only a few three-pounders. Meeting the Hornet, also a converted yacht, Lieutenant James

M. Helm commanding, and the tug Wompatuck, Lieutenant Carl W. Jungen, Young proceeded with them into the harbor, his own vessel in the lead, the Wompatuck and the Hornet following. Insufficient water prevented the Wompatuck from keeping her position in the column, and the Hist and Hornet went on, firing at a gunboat which had been sighted. No decisive results followed, though the gunboat was struck repeatedly.

The Hist and Hornet, with the Wompatuck, now turned into another channel and proceeded toward Manzanillo. When not far from the city, Lieutenant Young sighted nine armed vessels arranged so as to form a crescent and supported by batteries and troops. Undeterred by this vastly superior force, Young continued his course toward the enemy. As Dewey had done at Manila, he steamed along the Spanish front, delivering and receiving a heavy fire. The Hist was struck eleven times. One projectile cut the main steam-pipe of the Hornet, which disabled her so that the Wompatuck was sent to tow her out of action. The Wompatuck had also been struck, one projectile passing through her just above the water-line. Informed that the Wompatuck was able to take care of the Hornet, the Hist turned her guns upon a large Spanish pontoon which was equipped with six-inch smooth-bore guns. This was soon set on fire and destroyed. A gunboat was sunk, and a sloop loaded with soldiers which had poured a musketry fire upon the Hist was also destroyed. A torpedo-boat and several gunboats which held the right of the Spanish line were damaged. The American force slowly withdrew, and the Spaniards made no attempt to follow. The casualties on the American side were three men of the Hornet scalded.

The action last described occurred on June 30. The Scorpion, Lieutenant-Commander Adolph Marix, reached Manzanillo the next day. Accompanied by the tug Osceola, Lieutenant J. L. Purcell, the Scorpion dashed into the harbor and opened fire, but it was found impossible to destroy the gunboats, and the vessels retired. Reinforced by the Wilmington, Commander Todd, and the Helena, Commander W. T. Swinburne, the American ships determined to make a fresh attack. Three channels lead into the harbor. Through the southern steamed the Hist, Hornet and Wompatuck; the Scorpion and Osceola used the middle channel, and the gunboats Wilmington and Helena the northern channel. Keeping as much as possible out of range of shore batteries, the American ships concentrated their fire upon

Photograph by E. Müller

TORPEDO-BOAT WINSLOW

the gunboats, which soon were totally destroyed. When night fell on the 17th of July, there was not a Spanish ship in Manzanillo which could aid in the defense of the port. Weakened by these losses, feeble resistance to our occupation of the city was anticipated, and Rear-Admiral Sampson directed the Newark, Captain C. F. Goodrich, and the Resolute, Commander Joseph B. Eaton, which latter had on board a battalion of five hundred marines commanded by Lieutenant-Colonel Robert W. Huntington, to effect the reduction of the place. The Newark and Resolute were supported by the Hist, Suwanee, Osceola and the captured Alvarado, the last commanded by Lieutenant Victor Blue. A demand was made for the surrender of the city on August 12, which was rejected, and a bombardment of the shore batteries was begun. Earlier in the day, Captain Goodrich, through Lieutenant Young, had advised the Cubans of his purpose to attack the city, and in accordance with his suggestion the insurgents assaulted the rear of the Spanish position. Flags of truce were flying over the hostile batteries and blockhouses the following morning, and the captain of the port communicated to Captain Goodrich a dispatch from the Secretary of the Navy announcing the signature of the protocol of peace.

In order to isolate telegraphically Cuba and Porto Rico from Spain, the department arranged, before war was declared, to cut the cables landing in those islands. Insurrection in Cuba and frequent destruction of telegraphic lines as one of its accompaniments had forced the Spaniards, in order to maintain communication, to lay a number of cables on the south side of the island. Four cables connected Santiago de Cuba and Jamaica, one led from Guantanamo to Santo Domingo, and one connected Havana and Key West. Immediately after the commencement of hostilities consideration was given to a proposal to declare telegraph cables neutral, but it was finally decided to destroy all save that connecting Havana and Key West. The immunity of this last line was due, not to unselfishness, but to the expectation that by means of it we would be able to learn much of value. Our action was justified by events. Over this cable signal officers of our army at Key West learned of the arrival of Cervera at Santiago de Cuba. The Marblehead, Captain Bowman H. McCalla, who was later to distinguish himself at Guantanamo, and the Nashville, Commander W. Maynard, cut two cables on May 11 at Cienfuegos; the St. Louis, Captain Caspar F. Goodrich, and the Wompatuck, Lieutenant Carl W. Jungen, cut a

CAPTAIN BOWMAN HENDRY McCALLA

In command of the cruiser Marblehead during the war

cable at Santiago on May 18, a few hours before
the Spanish division entered that harbor; the St.
Louis and the Wompatuck unsuccessfully attempted to destroy the Guantanamo cable on
May 19, but later this task was accomplished by
the St. Louis and the Marblehead; while the
Wilmington, Helena, Manning, and Hist cut a
cable running between Manzanillo and Cienfuegos.   All these operations were conducted skill-
fully and gallantly, and in some cases under a
murderous fire.

The honor of engaging in the first naval battle
of the war with Spain belongs to the converted
yacht Eagle, Lieutenant W. H. H. Southerland
commanding.   The Eagle enjoyed no protection,
and her battery comprised only four 6-pounder
rapid-firing guns and two machine guns.   She
was assigned to duty with the division under
Commander B. H. McCalla which was stationed
off Cienfuegos immediately after the outbreak
of war.   On April 29 the Eagle lay about fifteen
hundred yards from the mouth of the harbor.
Anticipating an easy prey, the Spanish torpedo
gunboat Galicia, mounting two 4.72-inch breech-
loading rifles, four 6-pounder rapid-fire guns,
and two torpedo-tubes, with another small gunboat, left the harbor and started for the saucy

American ship. A third gunboat, which remained in the harbor, joined her sister ships in a heavy fire. In spite of the odds against him, Lieutenant Southerland made no effort to escape, but boldly returned the fire with his 6-pounders, the range at first being four thousand yards. When the range had decreased to twenty-two hundred yards, the Galicia and her consort turned and retreated into the harbor. Southerland received the commendation of his commanding officer, Captain McCalla, for conspicuous valor.

No description of the gallant work of officers and men during the war would be complete without a reference to the conduct of the marines landed at Guantanamo. Under the command of Lieutenant-Colonel Robert W. Huntington, the battalion, six hundred and forty-seven strong, established itself in the position best suited for defense and the protection of ships coaling in the bay. On the day after the landing, Spanish soldiers, concealed in the thick underbrush, opened fire, and continued their attack until June 14, when Huntington determined upon offensive operations. From Cubans it had been learned that the Spaniards had their headquarters about six miles away at Cuzco, which was the site of the

Drawn by Henry Reuterdahl

THE MARINES AT GUANTANAMO

A raid in the brush

only fresh-water well in the neighborhood. Concerting with Lieutenant-Colonel Tomas commanding the Cuban contingent, Company C, First Lieutenant Lewis C. Lucas, and Company D, Captain William F. Spicer, both under Captain George F. Elliott, attacked the enemy. In spite of the intense heat, the mountainous and tropical character of the country through which the march was made, and the fire of the Spaniards hid in the dense growth, the marines and Cubans forced their way and captured Cuzco. The assailants numbered two hundred and seventy-five, while the enemy was five hundred strong. In this engagement the marines sustained but one casualty — an enlisted man wounded. The Cubans lost two killed and four wounded. The Spaniards suffered heavily, having sixty killed, one hundred and fifty wounded, and eighteen taken prisoners. And these casualties were not the most serious part of their defeat, for they lost their camp and supplies and their well was destroyed. As the direct consequence, no further hostilities were directed against the marine camp or the ships in the bay, whereas prior to the capture of Cuzco the marines had suffered severely from Spanish attack, losing five men (one of them Assistant Surgeon John Blair Gibbs) killed and twenty-two wounded.

Thus the Navy, Marine Corps, and Revenue Marine Service were represented in gallant deeds. President McKinley, on the recommendation of the Secretary of the Navy made in keeping with the Secretary's pledge at the outbreak of the war, promoted officers who had rendered conspicuous service.[1] All these promotions were at last confirmed by the Senate, with the exception of the cases, referred to in a former chapter, of Sampson and Schley. The commanding officers, executive officers and chief engineers of the ships engaged at the battles of Manila and Santiago were all in this way advanced on the list at the same time. Then, that the department might provide for all cases worthy of promotion, a board of retired rear-admirals — Sicard, Matthews and Norton — was appointed after the close of the war, which carefully examined every record submitted. It recommended a number of advancements, which were made and confirmed. Not all officers were satisfied, but the board was disinterested and painstaking. The law makes " extraordinary heroism " and " eminent and conspicuous conduct in battle " the grounds of promotion, and, while there were numberless instances of heroism and of gallant conduct in battle, it was not in many cases possible for the

[1] See Appendix D for list of promotions.

board to lift them out of the high common range of faithful and ordinary discharge of duty into the extraordinary range contemplated by the law. If in any case a point was strained, it was in favor of the officer. Indeed, not without some force was the rejoinder of some of the disappointed officers that promotion had been recommended to participants in the battles of the war who did not come more than themselves within the strict letter of the statute; there may have been some errors of over-liberality, but, if so, they were on the generous side.

Hobson was advanced ten numbers and given the rank of captain. His men were not only given higher ratings than before, but also medals of honor and gratuities of one hundred dollars each. Some of the officers hereinbefore named, both in the Navy and in the Marine Corps, received advances in number on the report of the board above referred to, as did many others who, though not in the battle of Manila or of Santiago, yet displayed " extraordinary heroism " or " eminent and conspicuous conduct in battle " elsewhere. Lieutenant F. H. Newcomb, of the Revenue Marine Service, commanding the revenue cutter Hudson, was given a gold medal by act of Congress.

These advancements in numbers worked un-

II

merited hardship upon many officers who had no chance to achieve distinction and who were equally as patriotic and competent as those who achieved it. For such it was especially galling that after the war they found themselves in actually lower relative place on the navy list than before the war, reduced in rank and delayed in receipt of the increased pay that comes with regular rise in grade. In other words, the promotions made were at the expense, not of the government, but of the unfortunate officers overridden. After repeated appeals by the Secretary of the Navy to Congress, an act was at last passed practically providing that, when an officer had been or should be promoted for gallant conduct, those previously above him should not lose their respective numbers, but if, for instance, No. 10 is promoted to No. 5, he becomes an additional number and the original No. 5 goes up the list together with him. Thus every loss in rank suffered by any officer as above stated was made good.

I have entitled this chapter " Some of the Gallant Deeds of the War," because it is simply impossible to enumerate them all. To do so it would be almost necessary to name every officer and man. It is the fortune of great events that only those who are in the most conspicuous exposures have their praises sung; and yet not only the courage and spirit, but the merit of duty done and peril faced, may be just as great in those who are below the binnacles. Who shall say that the fireman sweating at the furnace in the bowels of the ship, or the commander taking his almost submerged and heat-stifled monitor day after day and week after week across the Pacific, is not as deserving as the chief who is in command when a booming victory is won ?

Nor were all the gallant deeds of the war deeds of martial prowess. Peace hath her heroisms no less renowned than war. There was nothing more gallant or inspiring than the rescue of the Spaniards from their sinking ships by our men at Santiago. Sampson says in his report: " The Iowa, assisted by the Ericsson and the Hist, took off the crew of the Vizcaya, while the Harvard and the Gloucester rescued those of the Infanta Maria Teresa and the Almirante Oquendo. This rescue of prisoners, including the wounded, from the burning Spanish vessels was the occasion of some of the most daring and gallant conduct of the day. The ships were burning fore and aft, their guns and reserve ammunition were exploding, and it was not known at what moment the fire would reach the main

magazines. In addition to this a heavy surf was
running just inside of the Spanish ships. But no
risk deterred our officers and men until their
work of humanity was complete." The Indiana
also " sent boats," says Captain Taylor, " with
surgeons on shore to the burning vessels to assist
in caring for the wounded." Captain Philip's
tender words, already quoted in a former chapter,
have become historic. Our later treatment of our
naval prisoners is especially creditable, and was
in the spirit of the highest gallantry. The officers, with Cervera at the head, were quartered in
the Naval Academy buildings on the delightful
grounds at Annapolis, and were there treated with
the utmost consideration, which he and they cordially appreciated and acknowledged. The sailors were taken to the navy-yard grounds at
Portsmouth, New Hampshire, and provided with
new and excellent barracks, the best of food,
medical attendance, and everything that could
conduce to their comfort. Their mother-land
could not have nursed or cared for them more
tenderly or substantially.

Nor, first among the heroes of that time, should
be forgotten the name of President McKinley.
In the bloom of his youth he had done gallant
and heroic service and won distinction in the
war for the Union — not for war's or glory's sake

but for his country's.   His was the same spirit
in 1898 and all through his life.   If ever head and
heart and conscience were, in the fear of God
and with prayerful sense of duty, devoted to
country and to fellow men, McKinley's were.
No president ever more embodied the common
sense and the best spirit of the people.   None was
ever in closer and more mutually confiding touch
and sympathy with them, and none has ever
had such a hold on the trust and cordially coöperating responsiveness of their representatives in
the national Congress.   He sought their welfare
in the expansion of their moral, educational, industrial, and commercial activities, and in their
peace and harmonious coöperation among themselves and with all the peoples of the world.
Peace everywhere he sought.   How beautifully
and successfully he cast — never losing an opportunity — the balm of healing into the wounds
of the Civil War, if any were anywhere still left
rankling!   The blue and the gray recognized in
him the president of their reunited hearts as well
as of their reunited States.   He strained every
effort to avert war with Spain.   When it came
he inspired into it every sentiment of generosity.
From his private purse, in which was little more
than his salary, he gave, unknown to many even to
this day, thousands of dollars to relieve the neces-

sities of the starving Cubans.   He was always on
the watch to send his message of good will to every
soldier in the field, to recognize quickly every
gallant deed done, and to help in every way to
lighten the burden and cheer the labors of the
campaign.   Wherever he could put the rosebud
of a kind word or act into any hand — and the
humbler and needier the quicker — he gave it
straight from his own.   He seized the first opportunity for a cessation of hostilities and for
terms of peace.   The whole atmosphere of his
presence and influence was benignant peace.   His
official life was one long act of heroism.   Merciful, pure in heart, peacemaker, reverent, sincere,
simple in habit, an ideal of home life, eloquent
and persuasive in speech, and wise and far and
wide seeing in the conduct of affairs no detail
of which escaped his ken, loyal to friends, kind
to all, in sympathy with every class, progressive
yet never giving cause for the fear of disaster,
how safe was the rudder of state in his hand, and
how, if we seek the elements of a true hero, he
embodied them!   How that noble and endeared
face still shines upon us through the years!

It is pleasant to recall the gallant conduct during the war of others than our own.   Among
these is Ramsden, the English consul at Santiago.
As soon as he learned of the capture of Hobson

and his men he actively visited them in prison, saw that they were supplied with bedding and good food, and secured their removal to quarters in the city. The Spaniards, who esteemed him and who were neither cruel nor vindictive, recognized his fine sense of humanity and were in sympathy with it. Though having a country home outside the city he stayed inside it during the siege, sparing himself no strain in caring for any sick or wounded. It was the sacrifice of his life, for he took a fever and, going away too late, died August 10, 1898, soon after his arrival in Jamaica. It was a fine instance not only of individual gallantry but of the better spirit of the age. After the war Mr. R. U. Johnson, of the " Century Magazine," suggested to me the erection of some memorial to this hero. A heavy bronze tablet, designed by Mr. Robert G. Skerrett of the Navy Department, was cast by it at the Washington Navy Yard and is now affixed to the house in Santiago where Ramsden lived. A replica was set up at the Naval Academy at Annapolis. The inscription was prepared by the Hon. Frank W. Hackett, then the accomplished assistant secretary of the Navy, always interested in good works. Lord Pauncefote, the English ambassador, wrote expressing the gratification which his government directed him to express at this tribute. The whole incident is an illustration of the sweeter chords that rise even out of the horrid din of war and prove that amid it all we are at heart in common human sympathy. The inscription is as follows: —

FREDERICK WOLLASTON RAMSDEN

Here lived during the Spanish-American War Frederick W. Ramsden, consul-general of Great Britain. He died at Jamaica, August 10, 1898.

The Navy Department of the United States, in token of his humanity to American naval prisoners, erects this tablet to his memory.

Then, too, could anything be more gallant than the conduct of the Spanish Admiral Cervera! His rescue of Hobson and his men from watery graves, his considerate treatment of them, his fearless heading of the forlorn hope of the exit of his fleet from Santiago, the order to execute which he bravely obeyed though he knew it probably meant descent into the jaws of death, his generous bearing at all times, especially after his defeat and during his sojourn among us here, made him almost as popular among our people as one of our own heroes. It has seemed to me that there was never a war in which there was so little personal enmity. The fine and devoted spirit of the Spanish queen-mother justly touched the sympathies of us all. Ours was certainly a gallant

and an intelligent foe.   The Spaniard has always
been a brave sailor and soldier.   His officers in
the recent war were men of marked courage and
ability.   They went to death in the most gallant
spirit of loyalty to their country and duty.   Many
of their reports, letters, and contemporaneous
and later writings on the various phases of the
naval and military situations are especially creditable to them and full of information and light
for us, excellent in description and statement
and spirit.   We have always been friends with
Spain and do not forget her help in early days,
but we ought now to be better friends for this
recent falling out and the quick making-up between us.   Spain has lost Cuba and the Philippines, but neither was of any value to her, as she
is probably well aware.   On the other hand, both
of them, relieved from ill-fitting incumbrance,
are swiftly moving on to better conditions, which
are already in full evidence.   As for our own
United States, it seems to have borne most of the
cost and brunt of the crisis.   Let us hope that
it will have its reward, not so much in the expansion of its territorial possessions as in the moral,
industrial, and commercial expansion of its influence, its institutions, and its republican spirit.

XI

THE PHILIPPINES, SAMOA, AND CHINA

In the Philippines, Samoa, and China, American sailors and marines performed service as efficient and valiant as in the war with Spain. Internationally, peace reigned in the territories named; in reality, a condition of war prevailed. Officers and men suffered and died in the service of their country in the Philippines. Officers and men were killed and wounded in Samoa to enable observance by their country of the obligations imposed upon it by treaty. Officers and men unflinchingly met death and sustained hardships and injuries in China while rescuing the envoys of all nations accredited to the Pekin government and while protecting the lives and property of the citizens of almost every Western power. Along the coasts of Central and South America our war-ships moved, protecting the interests of the United States and of other governments endangered by revolution. Officers have risked the loss of their commissions, to them more precious than their lives, in settling vexatious political questions; and rarely has their judgment been at fault.

Aguinaldo and other insurgent leaders, as well as their partisans in the United States, have endeavored to prove bad faith on the part of our country and its naval representatives with respect to the disposition of the Philippine Islands. William McKinley is open to no such charge. No promise of independence was given by authority of President McKinley. An express injunction was laid upon Admiral Dewey to avoid complications with the insurgents. This course was the only safe one to pursue in view of the lack of information under which we were at the time. Dewey's victory of May 1, 1898, gave us an immense territorial increment; few then appreciated its value, and public sentiment had not taken form as to its disposition. The sovereignty over it passed under the treaty of Paris directly to us by the deliberate grant of Spain, in whom that sovereignty was up to that time vested as it is now vested in us. Our title is the same as our title to Louisiana or Florida or Alaska. Under that treaty the civil rights and the political status of the native inhabitants of the islands were to be determined by Congress, and the result is they are substantially the same as our own. In every respect our faith has been kept.

Dewey has told of his relations with the Filipinos in such detail as to establish that if in the beginning absolute 'independence was thought of among them, he could give and did give no encouragement to that end. While at anchor in the harbor of Hongkong, the Olympia was frequently boarded by members of the Filipino Junta gathered at that port, " all very young," to whom and to whose statements Dewey attached no great weight. He first heard of Aguinaldo about April 1, three weeks before war began. On the eve of his departure from Hongkong for Mirs Bay, China, he received a cablegram from Consul-General Pratt, at Singapore, advising him that Aguinaldo was at that point and desired to confer with him. Dewey replied that he would see the man, but did not think it worth while to await his arrival. With the permission of the admiral, the McCulloch, after the battle of Manila Bay, brought Aguinaldo and thirteen other natives to Cavité. Dewey urged Aguinaldo to organize an army, but the latter, after a few hours ashore, returned disheartened and said he wished to go to Japan. Dewey revived his courage, and the next day he again landed and began to recruit within the American lines. He was ordered outside of the lines, but was given arms and ammunition which had been found at Cavité when that place was taken by the American squadron.

" Did you at any time, Admiral, recognize his government or his independence ? " Dewey was asked by the Senate Philippines Committee.

" Oh, never ! " was the response. ". . . Certainly, it never entered my head that they wanted independence."

Dewey's attitude toward the Filipinos was in full accord with the wishes of President McKinley. The first information the administration had of Aguinaldo's arrival in Manila Bay was on May 25, 1898, when the Secretary of the Navy received a dispatch from the admiral stating that Aguinaldo had been brought down by the McCulloch, and was organizing a force near Cavité which might render valuable assistance. This dispatch was immediately laid before the President, and within twenty-four hours the following reply was cabled : —

WASHINGTON, May 26, 1898.

DEWEY (CARE AMERICAN CONSUL), HONGKONG : —

You must exercise discretion most fully in all matters, and be governed according to circumstances which you know and we cannot know. You have our confidence entirely. It is desirable, as far as possible, and consistent for your success and safety, not to have political alliances with the insurgents or any faction in the islands that would incur our liability to maintain their cause in the future. LONG.

The above was the first instruction showing the policy of the President toward the insurgents; it was formulated and sent when the occasion arose that made it necessary. This declaration, made seven days after the arrival of Aguinaldo at Cavité, stated the policy of the United States, and no unauthorized representation, even had any been made by any one of our agents to the Filipinos, could affect it. So far as Dewey was concerned, no apprehension that he had been or would be indiscreet existed. In battle he had proved himself to be a cool, courageous commander-in-chief; in diplomacy, he had already displayed judgment and tact, and the President was willing for the time to leave the handling of matters in the Philippine Islands in his hands. At the same time, it was gratifying to the department to receive from him on June 6 a message stating that he had acted according to the spirit of the department's instructions from the beginning, and had entered into no alliance with the insurgents or with any faction. That the President might be informed in regard to the relations of the Americans and Filipinos, Dewey was directed to make a full report, and his reply utterly removed the fear which had been growing in certain quarters that the United States was in some way committed to the insurgent cause.

Drawn by Henry Reuterdahl

PROTECTING AMERICAN INTERESTS IN CHINA

The cruiser New Orleans coming to anchor in Shanghai Harbor

Foreign concern in regard to the fate of the Philippines was shown by the action of Great Britain, Germany, France, and Japan in assigning ships to duty in Manila Bay after the destruction of the Spanish fleet. Germany, the interests of which nation in the islands were comparatively of not much value, mobilized at Manila a force stronger than that under the command of Admiral Dewey. Her officers and men displayed sympathy for the Spaniards, committed breaches of international and naval etiquette, and showed disregard and contempt for the blockade established by Dewey, all of which gave rise to serious friction and might have led to an open rupture. The American commander-in-chief, however, compelled respect for his blockade, and gave it to be plainly understood that he would permit no interference with his rights. Mr. Joseph L. Stickney, a newspaper correspondent, who acted as one of Dewey's aides during the battle of Manila Bay, thus described Dewey's action when informed of the landing of provisions in Manila by a German cruiser. Lieutenant Thomas M. Brumby, Dewey's flag lieutenant, was ordered to present the admiral's compliments to Rear-Admiral von Diederich, to inform him of this " extraordinary disregard of the usual courtesies of naval intercourse," and to tell him that " if he wants a fight he can have it right now." This prompt notification was effective. It was followed by a disavowal of the action of the cruiser, and a declaration that it was done without instructions.

Aguinaldo was prevented from completing his conquest of Subig Bay by the German cruiser Irene, which took Isla Grande under her protection. The Raleigh and Concord were at once sent to that point. The Irene hastily retired and the Spaniards surrendered to the American ships. When the joint army and navy operations against Manila began on August 13, the German and French men-of-war, the latter being also in sympathy with the Spaniards, occupied a position northwest of the city, which enabled them to command the American station. The English and Japanese vessels lay off Cavité, not far from the American squadron. The feeling existed on board our ships that the Germans might fire upon them during the bombardment of the city, but if anything of the kind were contemplated — and let us presume that no such intention existed — it was perhaps blocked by the action of Captain Chichester, the senior British naval officer, in placing his command during the bombardment between them and Dewey. Captain Chichester recently described his relations with Admiral von Diederich.

"When the German admiral sent me word that he was coming aboard my ship to get me to join in a protest against Dewey's action," he said, "I looked up international law and spread the books out on my cabin table with the pages open and marked—all in a row—and when he came, I said: 'What can I do. This American admiral is so deadly right in all that he has done and all he proposes to do that if we protest we will merely show that we do not understand the law.' Of course, there was nothing to be done, and I did it."

Manila was virtually captured on May 1, when Montojo's squadron was destroyed and Dewey notified the Spanish governor-general that he would fire upon the city if the batteries defending it opened upon his ships. The city was not occupied by us at that time because Dewey could not spare from his squadron the force necessary for this purpose.

Before the protocol suspending hostilities between the United States and Spain was signed, it had become apparent that the insurgents were preparing to turn against us the weapons Dewey had given them. Dewey advised the Secretary of the Navy under date of July 26 that the most difficult problem to be handled by Major-General Wesley M. Merritt, commanding the army in the

II

Philippines, would be how to deal with Aguinaldo. The fall of Manila was followed by an insurgent demand for joint occupation of the city. Reference of this development to Washington was followed by an instruction sent to Dewey and to Merritt prohibiting such joint occupation, announcing that the United States must preserve peace and protect persons and property in the territory held by its military and naval forces, and declaring that insurgents and all others must recognize the military occupation and authority of the United States and the cessation there of hostilities. "Use any means in your judgment to this end," Dewey and Merritt were advised. There was no desire on the part of the navy or army to engage the insurgents, but the latter became more aggressive. Without respecting the proclamation of the President suspending hostilities, they continued offensive movements against outlying Spanish posts, seizing arms and ammunition and arming recruits. Around the American position at Manila they constructed a series of intrenchments. In January of 1899 our troops were practically besieged by the insurgent forces.

On February 4, 1899, the latter made their first attempt to drive the Americans into the sea. The navy coöperated with the army, shelling the insurgent trenches at points where they could be reached. From that time till the close of the insurrection American ships were busily engaged and coöperated with the army in patrolling the waters of the archipelago and cutting off war supplies sent to the insurgents from Hongkong and Chinese ports, and in making surveys and correcting charts for the benefit of trading as well as war vessels. The cruising of large men-of-war among the islands was dangerous, as was shown by the loss of the Charleston, which, on November 2, 1899, struck on an uncharted reef a few miles north of Luzon. From insufficient depth of water they were unable at many points to approach sufficiently close to shore to render effective service. Thirteen small gunboats, purchased by the military authorities from Spain, were therefore turned over to the navy, and, with the addition of those captured by Dewey, an effective mosquito fleet of seventeen vessels was formed. They were commanded for the most part by young ensigns and cadets, who displayed gallantry and, except in a few isolated instances, excellent judgment. The navy was the first to land a force at Ilo Ilo, an island of Panay, entering the town on February 11, a week after the insurgent attack upon Manila. A military force, under Brigadier-General Marcus P. Miller, followed later in the wake of the naval detachment and were thus enabled to inherit easy possession. But for the promptness with which the navy, to which the credit for the capture was due, had acted, the insurgents would have destroyed the town by fire. Between February 27 and April 4, Ensign Cleland Davis, of the Helena, with three marines, forming a colt gun crew, joined General Mac-Arthur's division operating north of Manila and " performed valiant service and rendered valuable aid to our troops." Sailors and marines destroyed at Olongapo, in September, 1899, a heavy rifle gun mounted and defended by insurgents. This point lies on Subig Bay, and naval experts claim it is the most advantageous site for a naval station in the Philippines. It was permanently occupied by our marines in December, 1899. The army and navy coöperating cleared the shore-line between Manila and Cavité of insurgents, whose fire had greatly annoyed our men-of-war. One hundred and eighteen marines, on October 3, 1899, served under Brigadier-General Grant in an assault upon the town of Imus, south of Manila. Three hundred and fifty-six marines, commanded by Lieutenant-Colonel G. F. Elliott, succeeded on October 8, 1899, in capturing Novaleta, which the Spaniards had considered almost impregnable. Vigan, Luzon, was captured on November 26 by the Oregon, Callao, and Samar. Captain B. H.

McCalla, commanding the Newark, received in December, 1899, the surrender of the provinces of Cagayan and Isabela, northern Luzon, and turned them over to the army. Five hundred and twenty-two persons, ten of whom were Americans, held prisoners by the insurgents, were rescued by an expedition, under Lieutenant J. H. Gibbons, fitted out from the Brooklyn. The gunboat Vicksburg, Commander E. B. Barry, participated in the expedition that effected the capture of Aguinaldo, and Brigadier-General Frederick Funston officially reported upon the invaluable aid thus rendered. Naval patrol of the island of Samar prevented the introduction of food supplies, and this, together with the destruction by naval vessels of supplies along the river banks, largely facilitated pacification.

These were some of the successes of the navy in the Philippines. There were also disasters. To prevent the massacre or capture and harsh treatment of the Spanish garrison at Baler, a town lying on a river of the same name emptying into the Pacific Ocean, Admiral Dewey, in the spring of 1899, instructed the gunboat Yorktown to effect its rescue. Upon arrival at the mouth of the river, Captain C. S. Sperry, commanding, ordered Lieutenant James C. Gillmore, one of his subordinates, to take a boat with a crew of four-

teen men and make soundings while another
officer engaged in a reconnaissance. Instead of
limiting his investigation to the mouth of the
stream, as intended, Gillmore directed his men to
pull within the entrance. He fell into an ambush.
His boat, riddled by shot, was sunk, and he and
those of his crew who were alive were taken
prisoners. For eight months these Americans
remained in the hands of the insurgents, suffering torture and hardships, and they were finally
abandoned without food or clothing in northern
Luzon. They were found and rescued on December 18, 1899, by a detachment of American
troops under Colonel L. H. Hare. While aground
at Orani, Orani River, Manila Bay, the gunboat
Urdaneta was captured by insurgents, her commanding officer, Naval Cadet W. C. Wood, and
several of her crew were killed. The remainder
were held as prisoners. An expedition under
Commander C. C. Cornwell succeeded in recap-
turing the Urdaneta; she was thoroughly re-
paired and has since done efficient service.

Foreign intrigue sowed seed of trouble in
Samoa, and it produced a harvest of blood. The
principal islands of this group are Upolu, upon
which Apia, the most important town, is situate,
Savaii, a less valuable island, and Tutuila, possess-

SURGEON GEORGE AUGUSTUS LUNG

ing the magnificent harbor of Pago Pago. Under
a treaty entered into in 1889 by Germany, Great
Britain, and the United States, Samoa was governed in accordance with native laws and customs
but kept under tripartite control; and the signa-
tory powers were bound to the preservation of
order. The United States was further interested
by reason of its possession of Pago Pago, Tutuila,
which had been granted to it in 1878 as a site for
a naval station. Malietoa, recognized as king
of Samoa, died in August, 1898, and, after the
usual funeral ceremonies, the election of his
successor in accordance with Samoan customs
occurred as provided by the treaty. The candidates finally narrowed down to two — Malietoa
Tanu, son of the deceased king, and Mataafa, a
powerful native chief whom the powers had sent
into exile in 1893, but who had been allowed to
return five years later to Upolu. In case of dis-
pute the treaty required the chief justice to decide who should occupy the throne. Mr. William
Lea Chambers, an American citizen, was serving
at the time as chief justice. Recalling that
Mataafa had been excluded from the kingship
by the declaration of Count Bismarck, with the
acquiescence of the other powers, in 1889, Chief
Justice Chambers declared him ineligible and
awarded the throne to Malietoa Tanu. The

Mataafan faction at once resorted to force and drove Malietoa Tanu and his followers to seek protection under the guns of a British man-of-war lying in the harbor. With the exception of German agents, charged with fomenting the rebellion, the personnel of the tripartite government sought refuge on the British ship. Our consul-general, Luther W. Osborn, urgently appealed for a man-of-war, that the United States might do its share of the work of reëstablishing order. In compliance with this request, Rear-Admiral Albert Kautz, commander-in-chief of the Pacific station, was ordered to proceed in his flagship, the Philadelphia, to Apia. He was instructed that the Samoan treaty was in force and not modified or amended, and that it must be his guide in any action he considered necessary to restore order in the islands. He was further instructed to act in concert with the majority of the representatives of the treaty powers.

Rear-Admiral Kautz arrived at Apia on March 6, 1899. He found a critical condition of affairs existing. Either on board the English war-ships or under the protection of their guns were the British and American consuls and the chief justice, as were also Malietoa Tanu and his adherents. Ashore were three thousand natives, well armed, who obeyed the orders of Mataafa. Following an investigation of the situation, Rear-Admiral Kautz called a conference of the consular and naval representatives of the powers. He notified the consuls that the chiefs engaged in the revolutionary movement must be informed that they must proceed quietly to their homes and respect the law, that the chiefs and their people driven from their homes must be allowed to return, and that the order of the supreme court conferring the kingship upon Malietoa Tanu must be obeyed. On March 11, the American officer issued a proclamation in which he stated that the consuls had agreed that the provisional government established by Mataafa and recognized by them in the preceding January had no existence, and could not therefore continue to be recognized. Mataafa and his chiefs were ordered to disperse and obey the provisions of the treaty.

The Mataafans started to obey Rear-Admiral Kautz's order, when the German consul proclaimed that the American officer had made a misstatement. It was his purpose, he announced, to continue recognition of the provisional government. Following the circulation of the German proclamation the Mataafan forces, on March 13, began an invasion of Apia at various points. On March 14 the British consul advised the senior British naval officer in the harbor that the rebels had entered and surrounded the Apia municipality and that practically only the beach was free. Many foreigners had sought refuge there, abandoning their property. In the hope of deterring the hostiles, detachments of American and British marines and bluejackets were landed and marched through the streets of Apia. A guard, under the command of First Lieutenant C. M. Perkins, United States Marine Corps, was sent to protect the American consulate; a guard of British marines was landed to defend the British consulate, and a force under Lieutenant F. H. Brown, United States Navy, was ordered to a point known as Mulinuu to prevent injury to a number of unarmed adherents of Malietoa Tanu.

Strategically, the positions taken by the United States and British detachments were decidedly weak. Surrounding the consulates was a thick jungle, which shut them from support from the ships, though within range of the latter's guns. When Rear-Admiral Kautz delivered an ultimatum to Mataafa requiring evacuation of Apia by one o'clock of March 15, an attack was made upon the consulates, but it was repulsed. Before the time limit of the ultimatum expired, a force of hostile natives embarked in their canoes and moved toward Mulinuu. To save the American and British detachments at that point from annihilation the Philadelphia opened fire and compelled the retreat of the assailants.

Hostilities were forced upon the Americans and the British coöperating with them. To oppose three thousand Mataafans, Rear-Admiral Kautz could only assemble two hundred and sixty men. Apia and its vicinity were cleared of the enemy. Malietoa Tanu was enthroned, and the municipal machinery of Apia resumed operation.

Learning that a camp of Mataafans had been established at Vailele, a short distance from Apia, an expedition was organized to break it up. Commanding the American contingent of sixty officers and men, including twenty marines and a colt gun, was Lieutenant P. V. Lansdale, executive officer of the Philadelphia. Ensign J. R. Monaghan, Lieutenant C. M. Perkins, United States Marine Corps, and Passed Assistant Surgeon G. A. Lung were the American officers serving under Lieutenant Lansdale. The British were represented by sixty-two officers, seamen, and marines, under Lieutenant A. H. Freeman of the Royal Navy. Between one hundred and one hundred and fifty friendly natives, undisciplined and indifferently armed, accompanied the foreign detachments. The expedition advanced in skirmish order along the beach beyond Vailele. It did not come in contact with the enemy, and, after destroying a village in which were stored ammunition and other supplies, it began the return march. Lieutenants Freeman and Lansdale decided to leave the beach-road and proceed to Apia by a road a short distance inland. While cautiously proceeding, some natives were seen in front hurrying toward the left of the column. The colt gun was turned upon them but failed to function. The gun was overhauled and tested, and the column resumed its march. It had not gone more than two miles, when in a place favorable for ambush it was attacked. The friendly natives became greatly excited, and their fire endangered the Americans and British. Lieutenant Lansdale attempted to operate the colt gun, but again it jammed, and he was compelled to abandon it. In an unfavorable position and under fire of a superior force, it was necessary to retreat to the beach. When the order for this movement was sounded the men scattered, thus preventing mutual support. Lansdale was wounded below the knee and could not walk. Ordinary Seaman N. E. Edsall came to his assistance, and while aiding his officer was mortally wounded.

"It is in evidence most clear," reported Captain Edwin White, commanding the Philadelphia, "that when Ensign Monaghan discovered that the lieutenant was wounded, he used his best endeavors to convey him to the rear, and, seizing a rifle from a disabled man, made a brave defense, but undoubtedly he fell very shortly after joining him, and the hostile natives, flushed with success, bore down on our men in his vicinity. The men were not in sufficient numbers to hold out any longer, and they were forced along by a fire which it was impossible to withstand. Ensign Monaghan did stand. He stood steadfast by his wounded superior and friend — one rifle against many, one brave man against a score of savages. He knew he was doomed. He could not yield. He died in a heroic performance of duty."

Lieutenant Lansdale and two American sailors and Lieutenant Freeman and two British sailors were also killed. Five American and two British sailors were wounded. When the survivors reached the shore, they passed under the fire of a British gunboat and were safe.

Shortly after this engagement a commission was appointed by the United States, Germany, and Great Britain to go to the Samoan Islands and investigate the situation. They were taken there by one of our naval vessels, and, as the result of negotiations by these powers, Tutuila and several smaller islands were, in the division then made, transferred to the United States. Pago Pago is regarded as the best harbor in the South Pacific,

and is in an excellent strategic position for naval
operations in that section of the world. Peace
and contentment have blessed those of the possessions there under our sovereignty, which has
been administered by naval officers.

Great as was the task the United States assumed when war began with Spain, it was hardly
of more importance internationally than the anti-
foreign or Boxer outbreak which occurred in
China in the summer of 1900. Hatred of the
West, generated by the presumption and arro-
gance and open contempt of its governments for
things Chinese, brought about the formation in
the empire of societies the avowed purpose of
which was to exterminate or drive out foreigners.
Outrages perpetrated upon Western and native
Christians, especially in the province of Shan-
tung, where foreign oppression had been particularly applied, caused earnest diplomatic re-
presentations to the Chinese throne in behalf
of strenuous measures for the restoration and
maintenance of order and the protection of life
and property. The government of China was
in the hands of a strong woman, the Empress
Dowager, who, by a *coup d'état* effected in September, 1898, had deprived the Emperor of
power and had regained control of the empire.

With her reascendency the reaction against Western civilization and its representatives spread. A society, the I-Ho Ch'uan, or, to give it its English designation, "Fist of Righteous Harmony," whence the name Boxer, received support from Pekin and attracted to its banner, "Exterminate the foreigners," thousands of recruits whom it promised immunity from foreign bullets. Considering the manner in which China had been insulted and despoiled, it is not surprising that the movement was national in character. In sympathy with the object of the society, the Empress Dowager evaded compliance with the demands of the envoys, or, if decrees were promulgated as desired, nullified them by secret edicts encouraging the Boxers.

President McKinley and his cabinet early appreciated the gravity of the situation in China and the effect disturbances would have upon Americans and their interests. Acquisition of the Philippines as a result of the war with Spain had placed us in the forefront of the powers dealing with far Eastern affairs. There were in China in 1899 more than two thousand American citizens. Our trade with the empire, in which the Pacific slope was keenly interested, was valued at almost $32,000,000, and Great Britain and Japan were the only nations which there had larger commerce. To retain China as one of our customers, our accomplished Secretary of State, John Hay, who has shown such great ability in the conduct of our foreign affairs, acting with the approval of President McKinley and aided by the prestige gained by this country during the Spanish War, induced the powers of Europe and Japan to join in a declaration to observe the " open door " policy in the Celestial Empire. This move of great national and international importance gave the United States a prominence in the East which it held throughout the Boxer trouble.

The interests of the United States in the Orient demanded adequate protection. Insurrection in the Philippines required the presence of a considerable naval force for patrol duty and coöperation with the army, as well as for independent expeditionary movements. At the same time unrest in China early in 1900 made prudent the stationing of a number of ships in her waters. To direct properly the movements and supervise the work of the two divisions into which the Asiatic fleet thus naturally fell, two flag officers were, with the approval of the President, sent to the East. For commander-in-chief the department selected Rear-Admiral George C. Remey, who had displayed remarkably good judgment

CAPTAIN NEWT H. HALL, U. S. M. C.

and executive ability while in command of the naval base at Key West during the Spanish War, and as second in command Rear-Admiral Louis Kempff. Before the arrival of these officers in the East the gunboat Wheeling was sent on April 2 to Taku. Conditions improved in the course of the next few weeks and the Wheeling was withdrawn. The improvement was but temporary. Operations of the Boxers extended almost to the gates of Pekin, and they even conducted their propaganda within the walls of the capital. Rear-Admiral Kempff hoisted his flag on the Newark on April 24, 1900, and one month later he was ordered to Taku. Before her departure for the Chinese port, the Newark received from the Oregon a detachment of twenty-five marines under the command of Captain J. T. Myers, United States Marine Corps. These were intended for service at our legation in Pekin. The Newark arrived at Taku on May 27, and found there the ships of other nations. On the following day, Minister Conger, representing the United States, and other envoys, believing that the Boxer movement had developed into open rebellion, telegraphed to Rear-Admiral Kempff to send a guard. Marines of the Newark, commanded by Captain Newt T. Hall, were added to Captain Myers's detachment, which was

II

landed with a company of bluejackets, a three-inch field-gun, and a colt automatic gun. The entire force was placed under Captain B. H. McCalla, the commander of the Newark, who had done good work at Guantanamo and other Cuban points during the struggle with Spain. The Americans were the first foreign troops at this crisis to enter the foreign settlement at Tientsin, reinforcing an English detachment which had been stationed there during the winter. The bluejackets and the field-gun under Lieutenant Daniel W. Wurtzbaugh were left at Tientsin, and Captain McCalla, with his aide Naval Cadet C. E. Courtney, Paymaster H. E. Jewett, the marines, the colt gun, and three bluejackets, pushed on to Pekin. The train conveying them also carried English, French, German, Japanese, Austrian, and Italian marines and sailors. As at Tientsin, the Americans were the first to reach the gates of Pekin. Having consulted with Minister Conger and seen his men properly encamped, Captain McCalla, with Paymaster Jewett and Cadet Courtney, returned to Tientsin. They arrived on the last train which came through from the capital.

The situation daily became more critical, and on June 4 Minister Conger asked Secretary Hay that instructions be given to Rear-Admiral Kempff to concert with other officers commanding naval forces at Taku as to taking measures warranted by the situation to eventually deliver Pekin. The dispatch containing this request mentioned the possibility that the legations might be besieged, railways blocked, and telegraph lines cut. Rear-Admiral Kempff was at once authorized by the Secretary of the Navy to take all measures that were practicable and discreet to protect the legation and American interests generally.[1] By his direction Captain McCalla, with forty-seven men and three officers, landed from the Newark and proceeded to Tientsin. This force was subsequently swelled to one hundred and twelve officers and men. The avowed helplessness of the imperial government and the insulting and threatening attitude of Chinese soldiers caused Minister Conger to wire to Rear-Admiral Kempff on June 9 that railroad communication ought to be opened. On the preceding day, the consuls and senior officers commanding naval detachments at Tientsin had held a meeting to devise means to protect the legations, but no agreement was reached. In the light of Minister Conger's messages and the known seriousness of the situation, Captain McCalla informed the consular

[1] Rear-Admiral Kempff states in a recent letter that these instructions were not received by him.

and naval representatives on June 9 that it was inadvisable to remain inactive, and he proposed to start for Pekin even if the troops of other nations remained behind. This announcement was effective. An agreement was reached that Vice-Admiral Sir Edward Seymour, commander-in-chief of the British Asiatic fleet, Captain McCalla, the Japanese captain, and the senior Austrian and Italian officers should start for the capital on June 10. German, French, and Russian detachments, unwilling that their governments should be unrepresented in an expedition of such international importance, joined the column when it arrived at Lofa, a point on the railroad connecting Tientsin and Pekin. It was under the command of Vice-Admiral Seymour, and comprised 2066 officers and men, of whom 915 were British, 450 German, 312 Russian, 158 French, 112 American, 54 Japanese, 40 Italian, and 25 Austrian.

The expedition reached Lang-fang, forty miles from Pekin, on June 13, having thereto met with practically no resistance. Here it was ascertained that the railroad in the rear of the troops had been destroyed and that the imperial forces had joined the Boxers, who attacked the column. The railroad between Lang-fang and Pekin had also been cut. With communications destroyed,

LIEUTENANT PHILIP V. LANSDALE

Executive officer of the cruiser Philadelphia, killed at Samoa

lacking supplies of ammunition and food, and encumbered with 264 wounded, the council of senior officers, presided over by Vice-Admiral Seymour, decided on June 19 to abandon the advance on Pekin and return to Tientsin.[1]

In the return the Americans were given the post of honor — the advance. Resisted at every point by an enemy, who received constant reinforcements, the movement was slow. On June 21 occurred an engagement which showed to the allied forces the bravery of American sailors. Intrenched behind the bank at a sharp turn of the Peiho River, the Chinese swept with their fire the embanked road along which the foreign troops were marching. " It is suicidal to attempt it," said an English officer to Lieutenant Wurtzbaugh, in charge under Captain McCalla of the advance guard. The danger was great, but Lieutenant Wurtzbaugh's orders were imperative. On the double-quick the men charged. Bullets sang about their heads, and some, unfortunately, hit the mark. Two Americans were killed and three wounded, among the latter Cadet Taussig.

---

[1] Rear-Admiral Kempff says that a further reason for abandoning the advance on Pekin is, " that in consequence of the capture by certain foreign forces of the Taku forts on June 17, 1900, the imperial Chinese troops came from the direction of Pekin, and made common cause with the Boxers against the Seymour Expedition, and made further advance impracticable."

Captain McCalla was wounded three times while with Admiral Seymour, but he kept at work till the whole force reached Tientsin. Early in the morning of June 23 the column captured the imperial arsenal near Hsiku, eight miles from Tientsin. Ammunition and food were found in the arsenal. Surrounded by a large force, it was decided to remain and to send for relief. This arrived on June 25. In the relief column were a hundred American marines, under Major L. W. T. Waller. Major Waller, with a hundred and forty men detached from the marine battalion at Cavité, had arrived at Taku on June 18, and on June 19 had landed and started for Tientsin, communication with which had also been cut off and which was in a state of siege. After severe fighting, Major Waller, in company with the forces of other nations, had reached Tientsin and relieved the foreign concessions. Immediately after the arrival of these reinforcements at Hsiku, Vice-Admiral Seymour returned with the entire party to Tientsin.

While Captain McCalla and his men were giving evidence of resource and courage under fire, Rear-Admiral Kempff was displaying good judgment and conservatism in connection with the international aspect of the situation. To maintain communication between Taku and Tientsin, Rear-

Photograph by C. S. Bradford

LIEUTENANT-COLONEL LITTLETON W. T. WALLER,
U. S. M. C.

Admiral Bruce, left by Vice-Admiral Seymour in command of the British naval force afloat, proposed to the foreign commanders that they take possession of the Taku forts, then held by Chinese imperial forces. Rear-Admiral Kempff properly declined to participate, on the ground that his government was not at war with China and that he was instructed to protect only American interests, especially against the Boxer insurgents. He was commended by the department for his wise conduct. Capture of the Taku forts by the other powers occurred on June 17, after a bombardment in which the vessels of the United States took no part.

The wall of silence raised about Pekin, the lack of information concerning Vice-Admiral Seymour's column, the siege of the foreign settlements in Tientsin, and the unrest which pervaded the entire empire aroused the greatest excitement and anxiety throughout the West. Few believed in those trying days that the Ministers were alive. Even in the cabinet of President McKinley and at large the feeling prevailed that they had been exterminated. The Secretary of the Navy alone held to the opposite opinion. He based his view on the absence of any evidence of their death and on the unwillingness, even as a matter of self-interest, of a government of the civilization of

China to permit the murder of diplomats accredited to it, who, by virtue of their position, are guests of the nation. Dispatch by Europe of reinforcements of ships and troops to China, while in part necessary for the protection of foreign interests, was dictated in large measure by the desire of each to guard its own particular interests from the others. In view of the critical condition of affairs, Secretary Hay deemed it advisable to enunciate the policy of the United States, in the hope of obtaining the adherence of other nations thereto. His note, dated July 3, 1900, sent to the other powers with the approval of the President and his cabinet, was the most important diplomatic move in the entire Chinese imbroglio. While stating the purpose of the United States to be the relief and protection of American interests, it reiterated the principles of Chinese territorial and administrative entity, protection of treaty rights in the empire, and preservation of the " open door."

More marines and ships and troops from the Philippines were sent to Taku, and on July 14 the native city of Tientsin was captured from the Boxers after a brilliant attack in which the Ninth Regiment of infantry and twenty-two officers and three hundred and twenty-six enlisted men of the Marine Corps participated. Following the death of Colonel E. H. Liscum, of the army, commanding the Ninth Infantry, Colonel R. L. Meade, of the marines, assumed command of the American contingent. In this battle the navy lost one officer and five men killed and four officers and fourteen men wounded. Further reinforcements arriving, another international expedition for the relief of Pekin was organized. Disheartened by the defeat at Tientsin, the Boxers made feeble resistance, and the allied force entered Pekin on August 14.

Relief of the legations was accomplished none too soon. From June 19, when Baron von Ketteler, the German Minister, was killed, until July 14, when Tientsin fell, they were subjected to systematic and fierce assault. From the latter date they suffered only occasional attacks, and on August 13, the eve of the arrival of the international expedition, a final and determined movement was made against them, which was fortunately repulsed. The United States legation lay directly under and was commanded from the wall surrounding the Tartar city. On this wall the Americans intrenched themselves. They held it in spite of repeated assaults by forces immeasurably superior in numbers and armament. On two occasions they were driven back and once compelled to abandon the legation, but, rein-

forced, they threw themselves upon the enemy
and retook the position. What Minister Conger
regarded as the bravest and most successful event
of the whole siege was an attack made upon a
strongly defended Chinese barricade which
threatened the station of the Americans. Fifty-
five Americans, Russians, and British participated
in this charge, and Captain Myers, who led them,
was wounded. The defense of the legations is
one of the most heroic deeds of history, and the
American people were gratified that their representatives conducted themselves with such gallantry as to earn the praise of all with whom they
fought and to whom they gave protection.[1]

The navy's work was not confined to the north
of China. Ships were ordered to touch at various southern ports in order to impress the natives
and reassure American and foreign citizens. The
effect of the presence of so many men-of-war
flying the flag of the United States was also great
in an international way, and it is not giving too
much credit to the navy to say that its work and
readiness for duty had much to do with the
prestige which the United States has had in its
recent diplomatic relations.

While the credit for the admirable work since

[1] See Appendix D for promotions for service in China.

Photograph by Gilbert

CAPTAIN JOHN T. MYERS, U. S. M. C.

the war in conferring on the Philippines the benefits of good government is due to the War Department under the intelligent and inspiring direction of Secretary Root, the navy was in at the beginning, and laid the foundation of the work. There has rarely been anything more creditable than the result. While there have been incidents to regret, the progress has been so rapid and so beneficent that it is an added honor to our country. Under the elevating and consummate administration of the American Commission, of which Governor Taft, so deservedly esteemed, is chairman, and of the seven members, of which three are native Filipinos, the forecast of President McKinley has been assured, and his policy vindicated. Civil government by civilians has been established almost from the first, the personal liberties we ourselves enjoy have been guaranteed and had, officials have been elected by the people, natives have been put in executive and judicial station, the chief justice and an associate justice of the supreme court being natives, a good revenue system has been adopted, the currency organized, tariffs adapted to insular interests, commerce stimulated, millions spent for public improvements, good roads made, sanitary precautions assured, free public schools opened with American and thousands of native teachers,

a civil service system applied, the question of reli-
gious and other land-holdings intelligently considered, and peace and order secured throughout
substantially the whole insular area. We have
done better in the Philippines than our own
fathers did here, who not only "subdued the
savage," but dispossessed and exterminated him.
We have given the Filipinos a government of
laws and not of men, as some mistaken good persons among us would have had us do by leaving
them in chaos. We have secured them individu-
ally the same personal rights of life, liberty, and
the pursuit of happiness which we ourselves
enjoy. We have made the individual Filipino
personally more independent than if his islands,
then unequal in their disorganization to the task
of a republican form of government by their own
disassociated peoples, had been left to what would
have been only a nominal independence and to
really the local and unstable government of the
various and changing forces and factions among
them which might be strongest for the time being. In fact, we have done more to make the
Philippines free and to insure their ultimate self-
governing independence than immediate independence so-called or an entangling and trouble-
breeding protectorate would have given them.
The question of immediate material profit to

ourselves may be an open one, but there is no question of the beneficence of our action to them.

In Cuba the story of our generous and up-building intervention — the noblest chapter in international helpfulness — is familiar as a household word. Here, too, since the war, the War Department under the same wise administration is preëminent.

In Porto Rico, however, the credit for the institution of the American system with its inestimable benefits belongs to the navy. Little time intervened between the close of the war and the establishment there of civil government, the assistant secretary of the navy, Charles H. Allen, having been appointed the first governor by President McKinley, to whom all these insular emancipations are now a historic monument. Without a hitch and with such marvelous success that the very absence of friction and incident has prevented the attraction of public attention to the splendid merit of the work, Governor Allen transformed that island in fourteen months into a condition of good government, of popular legislative control, of industrial development, of free schools, of improved roads, and of public and personal freedom, which, when at the end of that period he retired to private life, found its parallel only in the States of our own Union.

XII

SOME PERSONAL REMINISCENCES

THE cabinet of President McKinley was a body of earnest and patriotic men. The President, while guiding its counsels, yet directed them with an amiability and good nature which insured the sympathetic coöperation with him of these associates in his administration. There was, of course, never a set speech; there was no parliamentary procedure, and never a formal vote. Nobody ever "addressed the chair" or stood upon his feet. Matters were discussed in a conversational way. When the President had arrived at a result, he nodded to each member in succession, saying, "You agree?" until the last one had assented, and then wound the matter up by saying, "You all agree." Rarely was there any non-consent, though always full interchange of varying views till usually a common ground was reached. Cabinet meeting occurred at eleven o'clock on Tuesdays and Fridays, the members gathering at that hour each with or without a portfolio and one of them with

a green bag. Almost always at that moment the
President was having a last word with a group
of senators or representatives or citizens with
whom he had till then been in conversation, and
a few moments would elapse before the room
was cleared of them. Frequently some child
would be among them, and invariably in that
case the President would draw a flower from the
buttonhole of his coat and put it in the happy
little one's hand.

The cabinet is not an over-solemn body. Usually sittings were started with an anecdote or
merry word or bit of gossip. The President was
an admirable raconteur, and not only his previous
experiences but the incidents of his office were
attended with all sorts of amusing instances which
he would relate to us. Settling down to business
at the end, sometimes, of fifteen or twenty minutes, he would call upon the various Secretaries
in the order of their precedence. Mr. Sherman,
Secretary of State, whose sensitive and beautiful
face was like a benediction and whose legislative
record is that of the highest and most useful service, was then in that broken health which soon
after ended in his resignation and later his death.
Judge Day, who succeeded him, easily gave
evidence of the judicial quality which has since
led to his promotion to the Supreme Court. Mr.

Hay, who followed him and is still in office, has
made a career as Secretary of State of the most
distinguished character, and there is no more
brilliant page in the annals of the State Department than his.   He was a delight to the cabinet
board, full of humor, apt in anecdote, showing
in every word and phrase the cultivated scholar
without the slightest trace of the pedant.   Each
of these men rarely occupied much time with the
diplomatic budget, and readily dispatched such
business as he presented.   Then the President
turned to Mr. Gage, Secretary of the Treasury.
With the enormous business of that department
it was noticeable, as indeed was the case with
the other departments, how comparatively much
of it was disposed of by its head at his office and
how little was brought up by him for cabinet
consideration.   Mr. Gage had never been in
political life, and brought to his duties the business habits and the non-partisan spirit of a thoroughly trained, conscientious, and high-minded
man of affairs.   He had a ready wit, and in any
sparring in pleasantry always gave as good as
he got.

General Alger was Secretary of War, as kind
and generous a heart as ever beat.   There never
was a meaner conspiracy, for it seemed to be
hardly anything else, than what proved on the

resulting investigation to be a baseless attempt
to discredit him with regard to the supplies fur-
nished to the soldiers during the Spanish War.
If there was one man who would have given all
he had to make a soldier's lot happier, it was
Alger.   I used to think him a little sanguine, as
when, as early as the latter part of March, 1898,
the President would turn to him and say,
"General, how soon can you put an army into
Cuba?" and he would reply, "I can put forty
thousand men there in ten days." A little non-
sense now and then is relished by the wisest men,
and there was a kindly laughter in his eye as he
joked Secretary Wilson about his gray trousers,
or referred to my battered silk hat, which he
over and over again promised to replace with a
new one, but has, unfortunately for me, failed to
do so up to the present moment.   His successor,
Mr. Root, is justly recognized as a man of exceptional ability.   With the burden of the Philippines resting mainly on his shoulders, he had
practically to act in dealing with them not only
as Secretary of War but as Attorney-General
and Secretary of State, inasmuch as their administration, which devolved on him in the first instance, involved the most important diplomatic
and legal as well as military questions.   When,
therefore, his turn at the cabinet table came, it

II

was recognized that there would be little time
left for anybody else, especially as he spoke with
a trained lawyer's fullness. He was always lucid,
and maintained his positions with great force.
He, too, had a quick sense of humor, and added
to the gayety and sparkle of the talk.

Of the three Attorney-Generals, Mr. McKenna
was quickly transferred to the Supreme bench as
a distinguished judicial representative of the Pacific Coast; Mr. Griggs, just from the governorship of New Jersey, was a lawyer of marked
acumen and directness in the treatment of the
legal phase of public questions; and Mr. Knox,
appointed late in McKinley's administration, had
with clear convictions and judgment, a rare fac-
ulty for pointed and concise discussion. Of the
Postmaster-Generals, Mr. Gary, of Baltimore,
had been all his life a strong Union man and especially successful in the conduct of large manu-
facturing interests in Maryland; and Charles
Emory Smith, a lifelong journalist and an orator
of rare excellence, brought to our counsels not
only familiarity with the workings of his department but generous and progressive views on all
political questions. Next came the Secretary
of the Navy, and after him the Secretary of the
Interior, Mr. Bliss, one of the best types of
the New York merchant and man of business and

Drawn by Henry Reuterdahl

THE NEW NAVY AT SEARCH–LIGHT DRILL

public-spirited citizen. He was succeeded by Mr. Hitchcock, of St. Louis, equally distinguished in the same respects and just returned from the ambassadorship to Russia. Then came Mr. Wilson, Secretary of Agriculture, Scotch by birth but thoroughly American in every fiber. When Mr. Root finished his docket, the time was usually so far exhausted that we at the foot of the table used to suggest merrily that it would be a fair thing to begin, sometimes, at the other end of the line. Still, it often happened that Wilson, whose word of hard common sense always weighed with the President, did get in a sentence or two that went directly to the heart of whatever subject was on tap. The Department of Commerce had not then been established, but its present Secretary, Mr. Cortelyou, who was then acting as the President's private secretary, displayed in that capacity the striking ability for organization and system, as quiet and efficient as the running of a consummate machine, which later marked him as the man to install the new department of which he is now the head.

President McKinley was exceedingly companionable with his cabinet. He never seemed hurried or impatient, doing things in a thoroughly effective but quiet and never in a tempestuous way. He often took a member to drive with him, or to walk with him in the White House grounds. When he made extended journeys, like his trips through the South, the Northwest, and on the Pacific slope, he had with him as many of them as could go. On every occasion he put them forward to speak or for recognition. On those trips his comradeship was only the freer and larger expression of what it was at all times, even in the press of official business. Every year he gave a dinner to his cabinet officers and their wives, and each Cabinet officer in turn a dinner to him and the same company. These were delightful meetings, not formal but with all the neighborliness of provincial life. It could be said that at these times everybody unbent, if it were not the fact that nobody was ever at any time bent. The administrative circle was as democratic as a New England country sewing circle. Indeed, this might be said of all departmental and congressional Washington. On these occasions, too, we saw the habitual tender devotion of President McKinley to his invalid wife, which is one of the sanctities of the American home. It is grateful to get under what seems the hard surface of public life and to find there so often the homely and gentle currents of the common heart of us all.

During the summer of '98 the excitement was

intense.   Often of an evening members of the
cabinet would gather at the White House discussing the campaign in the Philippines and
West Indies, staying often beyond midnight.
There was constant telegraphic communication
in the executive apartments with our army and
navy officers, and in one room was a map so
arranged with little movable flags that a glance
showed the position of our several ships and of
our army forces.   On the night of the fateful
third of July we received a dispatch from General Shafter stating that " all the Spanish fleet
with the exception of one war-ship destroyed
and burning on the beach."   The President,
taking this dispatch in connection with one earlier that afternoon that the Spanish fleet had
escaped, translated it to mean that the whole
fleet had escaped with one exception.   I immediately took the other side — that the whole fleet
was destroyed with one exception.   And I ven-
tured to guess that when he got the report from
Sampson he would find that that one had not
escaped but had been overtaken and destroyed;
and so it turned out.

A cabinet officer should always have physical
vigor, — especially at such times.   It is not necessary that he should be particularly familiar with
the details of his department before assuming its

duties. He is really its representative in the councils of the administration, and does not so much represent it before the people as he represents the people in it. The great need in every department is thorough organization, the ability to secure which is an essential requisite in a cabinet officer. While he has the final decision and must keep a level head, he should give his bureau chiefs great power, but hold them to a correspondingly strict responsibility. He is pretty sure to be subjected to a good deal of criticism and now and then vituperation. We are a free and independent people, and every one of us is conscious that he could run any department of his government better than the head of it for the time being. This criticism is not merely that of the opposition party or of a partisan or sensational press seeking whom it may devour, but of friends as well. It is sometimes with a good purpose and sometimes with a purpose to make partisan capital or to hit a head or to raise mischief. But, on the whole, the cabinet officer fares well and in the long run gets his desert. Honest and even somewhat undue criticism does him no harm and helps keep his rudder true. There is one comfort to him and to every holder of a responsible post, and that is in the certainty that, no matter how much

Photograph by E. Muller

REAR–ADMIRAL JOSEPH BULLOCK COGHLAN

he is depreciated at the time of his service, yet a generation later — a little too late perhaps for his enjoyment — his successor, though very likely a much abler man, will be regarded as comparatively small potatoes. We are always praisers of past times and men, and belittlers of the present.

During the war, of course, I saw a great deal of General Alger, with whom my relations were most delightful, our offices being near each other. His responsibilities were overwhelming, and even he, with all his good cheer, was sometimes a little depressed by the hardships to which the army was subjected, the danger of yellow fever, and the necessary delays. I could not help rallying him a little after he had declined the aid of the navy in landing his troops. In the absence of other provision, there was no way of landing them except by the navy, to which he had to come and the services of which in meeting this necessity were handsomely acknowledged. It then turned out that the army also lacked means of landing its provisions and stores. Alger came in one day and said he was going to send a tug and lighter for this purpose, some of those already sent having foundered, and asked if I could furnish convoy. When I arranged that, he said, with a twinkle in his eye, " By the way, can't you lend me also the lighter and the tug ? " I remember rather a pretty scrimmage between him and Captain Mahan in the White House when President McKinley was present. The navy had been helpful in connection with the army transports and in landing troops, and especially efficient in destroying the Spanish fleet. The Secretary of War was complaining because we did not take the risk of blowing up our ships by going over the mines at Santiago Harbor and capturing also the city, which the army was undertaking to capture though the navy was bound to help, of course, all it could. Mahan at last sailed into him, telling him that he did n't know anything about the use or purpose of the navy, which rather amused the President, who always liked a little badinage. The Secretary of War, with his usual good nature, took the matter in good part. The fact is, he had the hardest burden of all upon his shoulders. The army, as he has stated in his excellent story of the war, was in a state of comparative unpreparedness, while the navy was in a state of comparative readiness. To call out and get ready for service more than two hundred thousand soldiers was a task which few have appreciated.

It is advantageous for the head of the department to have served in Congress. He is better

able to understand the demands which congressmen are under, representing as they do the wishes
of the people, and bringing to the departments
their constituents' numberless requests for all
sorts of consideration.   However burdensome in
their number and detail these may be upon the con-
gressman or the department, they are the natural
and just demands of the people at large.   In every
district there are scores of men who want government employment or have errands to be done in
Washington in the way of departmental information about contracts or relatives in the service
or pensions or what not, and there are scores of
bright, ambitious boys who desire entrance into
the military or naval academy or into the various
scientific avenues of government work.   All these
matters their congressmen present in all the various ways of the working of human nature.   The
word office-seeker has come to be a term of re-
proach, but often unjustly so.   Office-seeking is
no more limited to politics than it is to the pulpit,
or to teaching, or to any of the active walks of
life.   In every profession each ambitious member
of it is looking for a better place and more salary,
and resorting to every means to that end which
the office-seeker in the political arena resorts to.
We are continually instructing our youth that it
is the duty of the citizen to interest himself in

politics and good government, and yet if he seeks
a position under the government, although there
he can work to this end, he incurs the risk of
criticism. In other words, office-seeking is an
entirely proper thing, and only becomes reprehensible when it adopts objectionable methods.
The reform in the civil service has been not only
a reform in making political appointments depend
upon merit and not upon favoritism, but it has
also been an immeasurable relief both to the
appointing power and to the congressional representative.

During my time in the Navy Department my
relations with members of Congress were of the
most agreeable sort, especially with the naval
committees of the Senate and the House, at the
head of the former of which was Senator Hale of
Maine, and of the latter Representative Boutelle
of Maine, succeeded by Representative Foss of
Illinois. The services of these committees are
hardly appreciated in the glare of the greater
glory of battle. The pressure upon the con-
gressman for place varied very much according
to the locality from which he came. Districts in
which exist navy-yards or naval stations made,
of course, more numerous claims than others.
Employees in the navy-yards are constantly
pressing for better rating, and outsiders are

Photograph copyright 1900 by E. Muller

BATTLE-SHIP KENTUCKY

seeking to get employment in them. The reform rules which have been adopted in the navy-yards, however, now regulate these matters, and the Secretary himself cannot set them aside in the interest of any individual unless he is willing to violate his own rules and thereby give proof of the propriety of his own dismissal. His duty, on the contrary, is to see that they are enforced and that any violation of them is punished.

It was often interesting to see a member of Congress, perhaps himself a man of wealth and also, if he chose, of leisure, running his legs off to intercede for some watchman discharged for drunkenness or some janitor arrested for theft. On the other hand, all this shows how democratic is our system and how thoroughly the representative of the people is the servant of the humblest of them. There are some districts the representatives of which still seemed to be under the old-time impression that the whole government administration is a partisan machine and that it was a vested right of theirs to control the running of it in their districts and to run it in their own political interest. I remember instances where members from two districts contiguous to a navy-yard wrangled over the selection of a ship-keeper at two dollars per day, which office, till I put it under the labor rules, was the only one left out of them — left perhaps as a warning example of the old spoils system.

It was amusing, also, sometimes to read debates in Congress in which the severest criticism would be made upon the Navy Department for not sending more officers to sea, and to recall the fact that not infrequently some of the most emphatic orators were those who at various times had most vigorously, in individual cases, pressed the department to retain on shore officers in whom they or some of their constituents were especially interested. Naval duties require a certain proportion of officers on shore duty, and there are some officers who resort to every method in order to avoid sea duty. I remember one who had been at sea only two years out of ten, and even then in a soft berth where he did no watch duty. I ordered him to sea, and the very next day came an old personal friend of mine, a very leading member of the House of Representatives, who not only brought every influence to bear upon me to relieve this officer from doing his duty, but, although the case was so plain, expressed and for a long time bore resentment toward me because I would not let up. These, however, are only occasional instances, for Congress as a body, as is shown by its record of legislation for successive years, seeks the interest of the country at large, though sometimes hampered by the demands of individual constituents of its respective members. In debate, the orators of either House sometimes seem called upon, for home effect, to attack a department much more severely than their personal feelings and better knowledge would otherwise induce them to do. It struck me that heads of departments who had not served in Congress were therefore too sensitive to these innocuous assaults and too much annoyed by them, and that if they had themselves served in Congress they would have looked only to the general worth of the legislative work actually done and to the finer spirit of legislative helpfulness.

I remember one good senator who came now and then with the usual errands of his constituents, but was exceedingly sensitive if, complying with his suggestions, as was done in all such cases if practicable and right, they were referred to as requests on his part. He desired to have it understood that he never requested anything; and as it was a matter rather of form than of substance, it was easy to gratify him by use of the appropriate epistolary circumlocution.

There was also great difference in naval officers in respect to their assignments to duty. Most of them, with manifest propriety, simply accepted whatever duty was assigned them. Others directly or indirectly endeavored to obtain orders which they regarded as agreeable. Sometimes this was done in a manly way by direct letter or personal application to the department, giving the reasons for the wish expressed. But there were a certain number who, in roundabout ways and by securing interposition of senators and representatives and "friends," besieged the department and endeavored to manipulate their assignments. I was obliged to prepare a form of letter which in such cases I sent to officers, warning them that this practice would be noted on their record as indicative of demerit. Sometimes officers even in the upper grades came in for a word of this sort, suggesting to them that such a practice is not quite in keeping with the dignity of high rank, and that outside pressure from even the most "distinguished" and "influential" political and social sources in their behalf produced an effect prejudicial rather than favorable to them on the mind of the head of the department, who is bound to look at the interest of the service more than at that of any individual in it. However, these defects are small compared with the general rule of loyal and efficient service by the great body of the navy, in which there is to-day,

BATTLE-SHIP ALABAMA

more perhaps than ever before, a high standard of professional spirit and duty.

Social functions in Washington are apt to be accompanied with a good deal of sensitiveness, on the part of those participating in them, as to rank and place. A reception at the White House was pretty sure to be followed by heart-burnings. If an officer high in the army was invited and the officer of the corresponding rank in the navy not invited, or if a naval officer with a rich wife and social affiliations was there, while a senior officer with no such appurtenances was ignored, there was unhappiness. I remember that Roosevelt one day came to me laughing in his hearty way because one of his subordinates, loyally jealous for Roosevelt's rights, was very much aggrieved that while the latter, as assistant secretary of the navy, was not invited to some social administration function, a civilian clerk in the Navy Department, on a salary of some twelve hundred dollars a year, but whose wife was the daughter of a millionaire, had been a guest. It was about this time that the whole army was " mad " because one of its senior generals had a seat at the White House dinner not in the exact spot where he thought it ought to have been. Funnier still, a chairman of a leading congressional committee threatened never to attend another similar occasion because he was given no lady to take with him, there not being a sufficient supply of that article to go round, but sat crustily between two men. This was fun for everybody else. The great web of life in government as well as everywhere else has in it, here and there, its pettier threads.

The women are an interesting and constant feature in the business of every department, certainly in the Navy Department. Hardly a day passes that some wife or mother or sister of an officer or enlisted man or employee does not in his behalf visit the Secretary. Sometimes the interview is a pathetic one. An officer has been court-martialed for intemperance or breach of duty, or an enlisted man for assault or desertion, or an employee has been pulled up for improper conduct, and the offender is liable to reduction in rank or perhaps dismissal. The devoted woman, with disgrace or poverty staring her and her children in the face, is heartbroken. Or the errand may be to secure an assignment of duty suited to the domestic convenience, or to meet the necessities of sickness in the family. Oftener it is the mere matter of getting a pleasant or comfortable station where the associations or other opportunities may simply be more attractive for the officer or his wife or his girls, who wish to be in an agreeable social swim. Wives of officers who from the nature of their profession have no residence and therefore no means of securing appointments to the Naval Academy from congressional districts, plead with the Secretary to aid them in getting from the President an appointment at large, though generally they have already interviewed the President, for they let no chance slip. One cannot help feeling a genuine sympathy with a desire so natural and praiseworthy as the dedication of a son to the service to which his father has devoted his life.

All these appeals are made not only by personal interview but by correspondence, and vary, according to the character and manner of the applicant, in their method from those which are utterly selfish and unreasonable to those which carry a very strong appeal to sympathy. Sometimes the grounds urged will not bear scrutiny. A highly dignified gentleman comes in and urges in behalf of a boy who desires to enter the Naval Academy that he belongs to a family an unusual number of the members of which, he says, have occupied situations in the service of the government. "Indeed," he adds, "this young man has an ambition to be in the government service and no ambition for any other service." It is

II

hard to keep one's countenance and to refrain
from paraphrasing this sagacious remark by
saying that he is one of the numerous depend-
ents who prefer to be supported by the government than to attempt to support themselves.
And yet this dear man fancies that he has put
his case in a really eloquent and impressive way.

Another man, himself in the service, and having lived on a government salary nearly all his
life, clamors for more pay than he is earning, or
for some appointment or favor for his son or his
sister or his uncle or his aunt, on the ground that
he has given all his best years to the service of
his country. His view is not that the government has given a better return, as is very probably the case, than his abilities would have obtained him from any other source, but that the
fact of his having had a good position entitles
him to exceptional favors over other people who
have not had the same good fortune.

There are also many women in the clerical
force of the department. Most of them are
admirable clerks; but a very few of them are
shirks. And it is often the shirk, male or
female, who, while having the least merit, makes
the loudest claim for advance in place or salary,
for which all are properly eager, and is most
active in pressing congressmen and outsiders for

assistance. As a general rule, however, the whole clerical force, male and female, are, for the most part, efficient and satisfactory. Some among them are of superior ability, with qualities which, had they not become anchored in a government berth, would have probably given them good success in business life. They are intrusted with large responsibilities and often with those of pecuniary funds and expenditures, and their record as to these is a high tribute to their integrity. Though these clerical places are desirable, and the hours only from nine to four, with an intermission for lunch, there is always pressure for an extra hour in summer on Saturdays and for a half day before every holiday. There is, of course, no legal warrant for either of these favors, but I could never get the other heads of department to agree upon the correction of a violation of the law which had become a custom.

The navy had come to be a matter of so much interest to the people at large that there were constant demands upon the Secretary for representation of it in the various cities and towns of the country. Every State, of course, desired to have its name given to a man-of-war. No State was content with anything less than the biggest battle-ship. One senator came to me in great distress fearing that he would lose his reëlection because a ship of not quite that size had been named for his State; and yet Congress, and he as a member of it, had voted that names of States should be given to the class of vessels to which that ship belonged. Cities and towns were hardly content with vessels of smaller tonnage than the biggest. Senators and representatives were eager for these distinctions, and while the quest cost them a good deal of shoe-leather, I appreciated the obligation they felt to their great constituencies, and was in sympathy with their efforts in this and in other directions to serve the interests of their people, and — not to put too fine a point on it — their own. If there was a celebration on any coast or up any navigable river, the neighboring municipal authorities called for a naval vessel to receive their citizens on board and to send its bluejackets to march in the inevitable procession. The department was glad to comply with these requests whenever it could, for the navy belongs to the people who pay its bills, and it is a mutually good thing to have them brought in personal contact with it. It sometimes happened that a gunboat went so far upstream that it stuck in the mud, though full assurance and certificates from all the local pilots that there was ample water had been given to the

CRUISER ALBANY IN A HIGH SEA IN THE MEDITERRANEAN

department: there it was obliged to wait, sometimes a pretty long time, for a rise in the river.
The Marine Band, one of the best musical or-
ganizations of its kind in the country, was always
in demand, not only in Washington, but elsewhere. The difficulty in complying with this
demand is twofold: first, the need of the band
in its regular duties, and, second, the universal
protest from the Musicians' Union of the country.
The protest of the latter was put strongly on
the ground that the members of the Marine Band
are paid by the government at the expense of
the whole body of taxpayers, among whom is the
fraternity of musicians at large. It was urged
that it was not fair to the latter to be compelled
to compete with these favored few. The result
was that these requests were refused except on
occasions of immediate national character or occasions arising from some special appropriation
of Congress.

Aside from these public demands were the
numberless cases of personal calls. These covered every phase, not only of the Navy Department but of the whole political and social arena.
Delegations of excursionists, among whom was
pretty sure to be some old acquaintance, would
file through the Secretary's room in each of the
departments to shake hands and look at whatever

objects of interest the department affords: it always reminded me of Sam Weller's remark about
learning the alphabet that it was hardly worth
while to go through so much to get so little.
Sometimes a good turn could be done by taking
the visitor to the White House and getting him
a half minute with the President, whose patience
was unlimited and who always had a gracious
word and greeting. I remember one dear old
friend of mine, a clergyman, who came to me
hoping to get a place for his son. The son was
out of health and the father thought that the
climate of the Cape of Good Hope would be
helpful. He had seen that there was a vacancy
in the position of consul at some town there. I
was happy to go with him to the Department of
State, where the matter was looked up. It was
found that the place was vacant. I said, as I
could well say, a hearty word for my friend, and
the official in charge seemed to think that the
position could be had. There was hardly time
for a happy smile to fully illuminate the face of
the good clergyman before the official added,
" Do you know what the compensation is ? " and
on our saying that we did not, he informed us
that during the last year it had amounted to one
dollar and fifty cents, and that the place was
generally held by some local resident, although

for some time past nobody had been found who would take it. It is needless to say that the young man did not go to the Cape of Good Hope.

An amusing incident was a call which I had from a most worthy gentleman, who said that he had been detailed by the Civil Service Reform Association of his State to come to Washington and protest in behalf of good politics against a bill to transfer into the ranks of the regular civil service the clerks of the Census Bureau, who had been appointed without civil service examination and whose work was now finished. He said that this was utterly indefensible and an injustice to persons who had passed the regular examinations and were entitled to enter the civil service in their due turn, and who, if this bill passed, would be set back and many of them would thus lose their opportunity altogether. He said it was a blow at civil service reform, that we in Washington had no idea of the feeling which the bill had aroused in the home States, and that the principle of appointment upon examination and merit and not upon personal influence and favoritism must be enforced. As he rose to go, he turned back and said, in the most innocent and entirely sincere manner, " Governor, by the way, I have a boy about twenty years old, who is trying to do something in a business house but does not seem to succeed. He is a good boy and I want to get him a place. I thought that perhaps you or some of our friends here would have influence enough to help me get him a position in some of these departments?" I did not even smile. I knew that a more sincere and honest soul never lived, and that it was thé usual example of a man of genuine devotion to principle as applied to the world at large, yet utterly blind and unconscious when his own self-interest is concerned.

The professional reformer is sometimes disingenuous. I remember one who, speaking at a civil service reform banquet and overlooking the fact that the Navy Department was run with strict adherence to civil service rules, gratuitously charged that they were violated in a nearby navy-yard. I immediately wrote him to give me specifications of the misconduct, so that I might go for it. This request he refused, which I thought unmanly, but, after long effort and delay, I got the information through the national civil service organization and had an investigation by it, which showed the charge unwarranted and groundless except as a rehash of incidents occurring years before. But the false impression had been made and the good name of the Navy Department misrepresented in a respect

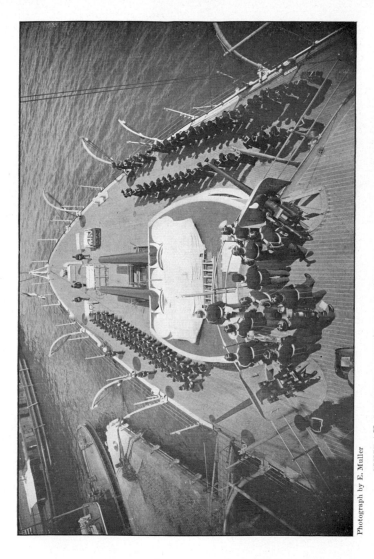

Photograph by E. Muller

SUNDAY MORNING INSPECTION ON THE BATTLE-SHIP ALABAMA

in which no other department, national or state, had a better record.

Since she was built, the Secretaries of the Navy have used the Dolphin for their official trips. Her service has been varied, once going round the world and thus discrediting the vicious report as to her seaworthiness that, evidently under political pressure, was made after her delivery by her builder. She served gallantly during the war on the Cuban coast, and afterwards in surveying South American waters. It was on board her that the Secretary visited the various navy-yards and the Naval Academy at the War College. The run down the Potomac, through Chesapeake Bay, into the harbor of New York, through Long Island Sound, into New London, Newport, Boston, and Portsmouth, and along the coast of Maine to the coaling-station at Frenchman's Bay, was always picturesque to the novice in naval cruising. The bugle-calls, the naval etiquette, the drills, the salutes, the ceremonious hauling up and down of the flag, the taps, the clean ship-shape decks, the groups of sailors in their blue or white togs, the foam of the cutwater, the visits and interchanges of courtesies with naval officers at shore stations and on board other vessels, the uniforms, the barges with their oarsmen, the reception on deck, the line of marines, the receiving officer and his staff, the music of the band, and all the incidents of naval life and discipline at sea, are pictures not to be forgotten. Comradeship with the captain and his officers and crew grows apace on shipboard; and the memory of days spent amid such associations — saddened as now and then a link drops out of the circle — is very keen. Captains Clover and Lyon and Commander Southerland, who were in command when these trips were had, and the fine young fellows with them, were as companionable as they were efficient.

The navy-yards were a source of interest and attention — scenes of activity, busy with men at work on the repair of vessels and the preparation of equipment, and enlivened with the spirit of naval discipline and regulation. They are no longer partisan political festers, but run — thanks to my predecessors — on business principles and under labor rules which make employment dependent on fitness and order of application, and retention on efficiency.

The Naval Academy, now grown to great proportions, was always a charming scene, especially on graduation day in the lovely June weather. Back came old graduates. Mothers and sweethearts of the boys gathered with their pretty

SECRETARY LONG VISITING THE BROOKLYN NAVY-YARD
DURING THE WAR

dresses on the lawn. There were exercises in the
chapel, athletic bouts in the gymnasium, a game
of ball, boats rowing on the Severn and the Chesapeake, a procession of the cadets in their tight-
fitting blue jackets with many buttons, the band
playing, the giving of diplomas under the spread-
ing trees, the groups on the green, the dancing
in the hall. Woven with all these things was the
thrilling thought of the future opening before
those bright, animated youngsters dedicated to
the naval service of their country, ready to give
their lives for its flag, full of the high-wrought
spirit of their profession and emulous of the fame
of its heroes.

Everybody who knows anything of an organized institution, though the head of it always gets
the credit or the blame of its working, knows how
much depends on his "right-hand" men, his clerk,
his secretary, his stenographer, and how quickly
these, if competent, master details and run the
clerical routine of the machine. I recall with es-
teem such men as my private secretary, Mr. Lewis
H. Finney, of a good Southern family reduced in
circumstances by the Civil War, not of my politics but an appointee of my predecessor, yet
retained by me, thoroughly familiar with the administration of the Navy Department, invaluable
as a clerical helper and in the delicate function of

meeting and satisfying the innumerable callers on the Secretary; or as Mr. Benjamin F. Peters, the chief clerk of the department, exact, informed as to every detail, holding the clerical force strictly to its work, quick to detect any unnecessary expense or abuse, always looking for methods of reform in business administration, and not popular with those inclined to shirk or waste, as no faithful public servant ever is. Two stenographers from the Secretary's desk, Mr. Harold C. Snyder and Mr. Walter A. Greer, fine fellows and laudably ambitious, passed the required examinations and got commissions, one as an officer in the Marine Corps, and the other as assistant paymaster in the navy. Nor can I forget, as a type of the best character of his race, the colored messenger, Morissey S. Koonce, whose alertness and intelligence met every requirement and whose spare moments were devoted to study for entrance into the civil service, the examinations of which he at last passed, thus going on the clerical list with all its opportunities now before him.

During the war there were many instances of individual generosity, like that of Miss Helen M. Gould, who gave at one time a hundred thousand dollars to the public service. Two or three valuable yachts were loaned without compensation to the government and used as auxiliary

HON. THEODORE ROOSEVELT

Assistant Secretary of the Navy, 1897–1898

naval vessels. One rich yacht-owner tendered his vessel, but accompanied the tender with the request, which made its acceptance impossible, that he, though a civilian, be appointed its commander, and that a steam engineer of his own be put in charge, with other like conditions. He really seemed to regard it as a grievance that he was not given a command with all the accompanying responsibilities and honors which even many naval officers, who had been in training for years, had not yet reached. Now and then came personal threats, not of course in personal interviews but by letter. These generally gave an interval of from three to ten days as the limit of the miserable life of the Secretary who was a disgrace to his country and would be made to feel the vengeance of the writer.

Mr. Roosevelt was an interesting personality as assistant secretary of the navy, as, indeed, he is in any capacity. There were several candidates for the place, which President McKinley allowed me to fill. In May, 1897, on the retirement of Mr. McAdoo, an excellent official under the previous administration, who had consented to hold over till that time, I selected Mr. Roosevelt who had had, and indeed has had to this day, a hearty interest in the navy. His activity was characteristic. He was zealous in the work of

putting the navy in condition for the apprehended
struggle. His ardor sometimes went faster than
the President or the department approved. Just
before the war, when the Spanish battle-fleet was
on its way here, he as well as some naval officers,
regarding that as a cause of war, approved of
sending a squadron to meet it without waiting
for a more formal declaration of war. He worked
indefatigably, frequently incorporating his views
in memoranda which he would place every morning on my desk. Most of his suggestions had,
however, so far as applicable, been already adopted
by the various bureaus, the chiefs of which were
straining every nerve and leaving nothing not
done. When I suggested to him that some future historian reading his memoranda, if they
were put on record, would get the impression
that the bureaus were inefficient, he accepted the
suggestion with the generous good nature which
is so marked in him. Indeed, nothing could be
pleasanter than our relations. He was heart and
soul in his work. His typewriters had no rest.
He, like most of us, lacks the rare knack of
brevity. He was especially stimulating to the
younger officers who gathered about him and
made his office as busy as a hive. He was especially helpful in the purchasing of ships and in
every line where he could push on the work of

preparation for war. Almost as soon, however, as it was declared, he resigned the assistant-secretaryship of the navy to accept the lieutenant-colonelcy of the Rough Rider regiment in the army. Together with many of his friends, I urged him strenuously to remain in the navy, arguing that he would there make a signal reputation, and that to go into the army would be only to fight mosquitoes on the Florida sands or fret in camp at Chickamauga. How right he was in his prognosis and how wrong we were in ours, the result has shown. He took the straight course to fame, to the governorship of New York and to the presidency of the United States. He has the dash of Henry of Navarre without any of his vices.

His room in the Navy Department after his decision to enter the army, which preceded for some time his resignation as assistant secretary, was an interesting scene. It bubbled over with enthusiasm, and was filled with bright young fellows from all over the country, college graduates and old associates from the western ranches, all eager to serve with Roosevelt. The Rough Rider uniform was in evidence; it climbed the steps of the Navy Department; it filled its corridors; guns, uniforms, all sorts of military traps, and piles of papers littered the assistant secretary's room, but it was all the very inspiration of young manhood.

Mr. Roosevelt had an admirable successor in Mr. Charles H. Allen, whose characteristics were thorough business training, special aptness for his work, complete system, and that orderly poise which makes the executive administration run like a well-oiled machine. He displayed also such large ability and grasp that President McKinley, with the immediate hearty approval of the members of the cabinet, to all whom Mr. Allen had become well known, selected him to be the first insular governor after the war. How well he discharged this important duty and set the example of insular government has been stated in a previous chapter. After him Mr. Frank W. Hackett became assistant secretary. He had served in the navy during the Civil War. A native of Portsmouth, New Hampshire, he was familiar with navy-yards, and brought to his position naval experience, the ability of a trained lawyer, and a keen interest in the navy. He was especially devoted to the maintenance of its prestige and high character. The present assistant secretary, Mr. Darling, who was appointed in my time, is another instance of fortunate selection. His judicial experience, his decision of character, his straightforward good sense and

HON. CHARLES H. ALLEN
Assistant Secretary of the Navy 1898–1900

business capacity, make him in the department a safe reliance to his chief and a prop of steadiness in naval administration.

An important feature in the life of the Secretary is his relation with the press. The press associations and the great city dailies maintain at the Navy Department representatives who gather all the news of interest. These men are some of the great body of newspaper correspondents at Washington who exercise a very responsible influence upon public opinion, and for the integrity, intelligence and acumen which characterize most of whom one feels great respect and admiration. On the eve of the war and during the war the department was crowded daily by newspaper men. When trusted with confidential information, as was sometimes desirable in the public interest, they did not violate the trust. News which they obtained not in a confidential way but by their own push they published, sometimes to the annoyance of the department; and such publications might, with an enterprising enemy, have in some cases proved injurious. For instance, when the Flying Squadron, upon the approach of Cervera's fleet, was ordered from Hampton Roads to Key West, the cruiser Minneapolis was detached to cruise off the Bahamas in order to watch for the Spanish vessels. This order was known to only five men in the department, yet the next morning it was published in a New York daily and thus might have become known to the Spanish authorities. Such occurrences were, however, counterbalanced by the efforts of the press to assist the government. Any information of value obtained by its correspondents was at once given to the department. The bright young man who ferreted out the above-mentioned orders to the Minneapolis helped in turn by knowingly giving misleading information as to certain naval plans the real tenor of which it was desirable to conceal. Such was the case of a press publication of June 27, that a squadron would sail immediately for the coast of Spain, the object of this announcement being to induce the return of the Spanish fleet which under Camara had started for the Philippines.

I was satisfied that it was best to be as accessible as possible to the members of the press. It was easy to arrange an hour when they called upon me to receive such news as I could give them. The department certainly lost nothing and gained the opportunity of giving information to the public, while the newspaper men were glad to have considerate treatment. They represented the public, and the public were entitled to all proper information. These grew to be very pleasant occasions, and I came to value the friendship as well as the intelligence of many of these members of the press. Among them was Mr. Edwin M. Hood, who represented the Associated Press, one of the most careful and conscientious men I ever met. His suggestions were valuable because always sound and disinterested. Mr. Richard V. Oulahan, of the New York "Sun," was a man of absolute trustworthiness and fine ability, whose full and luminous report of the Schley Court of Inquiry is a model of accuracy and fairness. Mr. John Callan O'Laughlin, of the New York "Herald," it seemed to me, never slept; no item of information, however recondite, ever escaped his keen eyes, and he was invaluable to his paper and often of helpfulness to the department.

One of the significant facts in modern life, certainly in regard to the navy in my time, is the publication of so many things that, as Josh Billings says, " ain't so." Not merely do these errors occur in the press proper, but in the more formal statements and speeches and narratives of public writers and speakers. I remember a distinguished statesman saying in a speech at a banquet in January, 1899, that, when the Maine was destroyed, there " was not on American ships or in the ordnance depots in the United States two rounds of powder per gun at that time. I may tell you," said he, " of the run of a sealed express train across the continent, the contents of which train no one outside of Washington, and only two there, knew. It had the right of way over all other trains. When it reached San Francisco, its cargo was transferred to a waiting steamer which raced to Honolulu. There the steamer Baltimore was waiting, no one knew for what. The cargo was shifted to the Baltimore, which carried it to Hongkong, and on April 23 the cargo was distributed among the American war-ships there, and Dewey had the ammunition he wanted. On April 24 he got his orders to sail for Manila. That ammunition on May Day awoke echoes in Manila Bay that were heard around the world and took from Spain an empire."

This was picturesque, but the orator was entirely misinformed. The Asiatic Squadron, without the ammunition received from the Baltimore, was already in condition to go into battle, and during the battle only a third of its ammunition was expended. The special fast train referred to, instead of carrying the ammunition which woke the echoes of Manila Bay on May Day, did not start from Harrisburg until two months later, on the 30th of June. It was the only train-load of ammunition sent West, and the object was to

THE NEW BATTLE-SHIP MAINE

Photograph by E. Muller

form at the navy-yard near San Francisco a large
reserve supply of ammunition for the Pacific
headquarters.   Indeed, Admiral O'Neil, chief of
the Bureau of Ordnance, on having his attention
called to this statement, reported that " one hundred and seven Asiatic vessels and fourteen new
commissioned vessels were supplied with complete outfits of ammunition, and a good reserve
supply was maintained at the principal naval
stations, so that at no time either before or during the war can it be said that the navy was so
short of ammunition that it could not at any time
have been called into active operation."

This is only an example of the innumerable
instances of misrepresentation which writers and
speakers, when not under the compulsion of
responsible statement, are led into making, not
with deliberate intent to mislead, but from an
overstock of misinformation.   It seems not too
much to say that often such public assertions are
evidence only of their own incorrectness or ex-
aggeration, and should always be taken with a
large grain of salt.   Experience in courts of justice has proved that no evidence is of much value
which has not been subjected to a searching
cross-examination.   Against the errors of statement irresponsibly made there is practically no
safeguard.

It at first seems a little incongruous that the
Secretary of the Navy has, as a general rule,
been a man who, when appointed, knew little or
nothing about naval matters.   This is the foundation of the threadbare story which has been
told of every Secretary in succession, that on going aboard a man-of-war he threw up his hands
and said, " Why, the darned thing is holler, ain't
it ? "   But there is a principle underlying this
rule.   Ours is a civil and not a military government.   The President is a civilian, and, if he has
had military experience, it is an incident in his
availability as a presidential candidate rather than
an element in his qualifications for the presidential office.   The heads of the Army and Navy
departments are civilians.   The fundamental
principle of our Constitution is that the military
is subordinate to the civil function.   Then, too,
as a matter of expediency as well as of principle,
it is better that the head of each department
should enter upon his duties with an open mind
and without the possible bias of prejudice or
favoritism which might come from having been
himself a lifelong member of the body over which
he is placed.   There must of course be the ex-
pert and professional knowledge of the trained
naval officer; there must be experience with
ships and navy-yards, with seamen and marines,

and with all the details of naval life; but these are amply supplied by the men who are called around the Secretary and placed by him in charge of the various bureaus of administration which have been described in former chapters, and the merit of the services of the chiefs of which has been heretofore acknowledged with the warm appreciation of one who has seen and felt their competency and devotion. The present general system of the administration of the Naval Department, as it has now existed for many years, has stood the test of all that time, including two recent wars and the upbuilding of the New Navy during the last two decades. It is possible that some better system might be devised, but with the constant improvements in details which will incidentally attend it in the future as has been the case in the past, no better system in general outline has been or is likely to be suggested. Certainly no change should be made which, while seeming to maintain the present relation of the navy to a civilian head in form, will displace it in fact. For this reason it has seemed to me that the general staff, which, so long as it is subject to appointment and control by the Secretary, as originally instituted by me, is a very valuable adjunct in insuring preparedness for war, should not be put by legislative enactment beyond immediate civilian control. Certainly no such act should be passed with reference to the navy as was passed in the last Congress in regard to the general staff of the army, which makes the chief of that staff the immediate head of the various bureaus of the War Department and practically gives him the control of them. Such an enactment with regard to the navy would naturally be followed by efforts for fixed tenure of office and for steadily enlarging power. It might tend to an undue increase of expenditures, which are already necessarily great, by committing them to an official who is permanently identified with only his own profession and is not under the responsibility of a civilian member of a general administration which is directly accountable to the legislative branch of the government and is subject to an early return to the criticism of popular elections. It is also likely to tend to professional jealousy on the part of naval officers toward one of their own number exercising the function of Secretary, while there is none toward a civilian exercising that function who goes utterly out of sight after a short term. If there is under the present system sometimes a little soreness on their part toward the Secretary, as of course there now and then is, they can take it out by growling and

Photograph by E. Muller

TORPEDO-BOAT MORRIS

calling him an uncomplimentary name, but they have, perhaps for that reason, no jealousy of one with whom they can have no question of permanent rank. Command of a ship or fleet is different from the command of the whole navy. The former gives its possessor necessary and readily accepted control over his immediate subordinates for a limited period and within a limited range, the latter over the naval fortunes, the assignments to continuous duty, the whereabouts on the face of the earth of every officer in the service.

To be sure, the Army Act above referred to gives this supervision to the chief of staff " under the direction of the President, or of the Secretary under the direction of the President." But with a chief of staff well in the saddle, it is easy to see how slight a check upon his mastery this provision would be, especially hereafter when a new Secretary comes in and is unconsciously subordinated to what he is led to regard as the customary order of things. Besides, the act will be a stimulus to the chief of staff to hereafter seek always direct communication with the President; and a President with aggressive force would easily come to deal directly with the official who by such a law is made the real working head of all the bureaus and machinery of the department.

Under such circumstances the Secretary could hardly fail to lapse into a figurehead in the administration of the navy and really to have no other function than to sit in an advisory capacity at the cabinet table.   Precedent quickly hardens into an inflexible system, and the first step should not be taken towards a military head of any department of the government.

APPENDIX

APPENDIX

A

LETTER OF SECRETARY LONG TO PRESIDENT McKIN-
LEY WITH REGARD TO THE ALLEGED "PERSECU-
TION OF ADMIRAL SCHLEY."

NAVY DEPARTMENT.
WASHINGTON, July 3, 1899.

DEAR MR. PRESIDENT : —

Senator McComas advises me that some gentlemen in
Baltimore have expressed to him by telegram a desire
for an interview with you with reference to what they
term "the persecution of Admiral Schley." I understand
this means his persecution by the Navy Department. If
so, such complaint is so absolutely unfounded and, also,
so entirely contrary to the truth that I should be glad to
be present if any charge is made, so that the facts can be
stated.

The Navy Department has, from the first, been especially considerate with regard to this officer. At the time
the Flying Squadron was formed, although Commodore
Schley was at the foot of the list of commodores, the department selected him for the command. You will remember that when I suggested his name you were yourself
inclined to question the selection. It gave him a command which was especially desirable, and to which any
one of his seniors might have felt entitled. He expressed
great satisfaction when I announced this appointment to

him and very cordially accepted it, expressing his pleasure at this service in the Atlantic waters under the commander-in-chief.

When the Spanish fleet under Cervera threatened our
shores, Commodore Schley was given a chance with the
Flying Squadron to go in search of the enemy; and here
again the department gave him one of the best opportunities of the war, and he had an independent command
from that time until the 1st of June, when the commander-in-chief took command. You are aware, of course,
that during this time of his independent command his
administration of it was not satisfactory to you or to the
department. There was delay in ascertaining whether
Cervera's fleet was at Cienfuegos, this fact not having
been ascertained during the several days when Commodore Schley had opportunity to ascertain it — indeed, not
until Captain McCalla joined him and immediately and
easily ascertained that the Spanish fleet was not there.
Commodore Schley's later approach to Santiago and his
exceedingly unfortunate and unnecessary turning back
when within twenty miles of that port; his acknowledged
and unwarranted disobedience of orders in so doing ; his
retreat for a day or two back toward Key West; his claim
of a lack of coal, when the records show from six to twelve
days' supply on board every ship, and when, if there was
coal enough to go hundreds of miles back to Key West,
there was certainly enough to go to Santiago, as was
shown when he again changed his mind — this time for
the better — and went there. All these things show
what I think he would now acknowledge to have been a
very great mistake and what, had the facts been fully
known at the time, would undoubtedly have been regarded as cause for relieving him from command, if not
for further disciplinary proceedings. You will remember

that when word came to you of this backward step of his, which was the only backward step on the part of the navy during the war, with what anxiety and gloom you were oppressed. Inasmuch, however, as Commodore Schley's independent command terminated at that time, and a month later the battle of Santiago, in which he participated, was fought and a glorious victory secured, the department felt that no action of a disciplinary character was necessary. The department, therefore, recommended the promotion of, and you promoted, subject to future confirmation by the Senate, all the commanding officers engaged in that combat, the commander-in-chief having the first promotion and Commodore Schley, as next in command, having the second, and so on. Thus far, certainly, it is difficult to see how there has been any persecution by the Navy Department or anything but the most considerate action toward Admiral Schley. Since that time the department has taken absolutely no action and expressed no opinion with reference to this case except in the following instances: —

First. In February last the Senate asked for the records in Admiral Schley's case. These were prepared solely from the official reports and given simply as required. In order that there might be no mistake or omission, the department appointed a board of three officers to collate them, and put upon this board Admiral Schley's own flag lieutenant, who certified to their correctness.

Second. A controversy arose recently in the newspapers, and entirely outside of the department, as to a colloquy said to have occurred at the battle of Santiago between Commodore Schley and his navigator, Lieutenant Hodgson. One newspaper repeatedly published this colloquy, claiming it to have been given by Lieutenant Hodgson. Later, in another paper, appeared a letter di-

rected from Lieutenant Hodgson to Admiral Schley deny-
ing that the colloquy published had occurred. It was then
published in the first paper, on the alleged evidence of
another officer, that Lieutenant Hodgson had stated that
such a colloquy had occurred. Under these circumstances
there arose a case in which it appeared that either one
or the other of the two naval officers had publicly made
a false statement in a matter affecting the navy. As this,
if unexplained, tended to discredit and scandalize the
service, it became necessary, as usual in such cases, to
call for an explanation. Both officers were, therefore,
called upon by the department to make explanations, the
result of which was that Lieutenant Hodgson stated that
what he meant by his letter of denial was that no colloquy
in the exact terms published had occurred, while, in fact,
the substance of the colloquy was substantially true. The
further fact was brought out that with his letter of absolute denial to Admiral Schley he also sent an explanatory
letter to the effect that this denial was only a denial of
the colloquy as published, but that the substance of the
colloquy was correct. Lieutenant Hodgson had already
previously to this sent a similar explanatory letter to
Admiral Schley.

The action of the department with reference to Lieutenant Hodgson in this matter, as will therefore readily
be seen, was the action which is ordinarily taken by the
department to give an officer an opportunity to explain
what, unexplained, might subject him to a charge of
unbecoming statement or conduct. The question might
arise whether the department should not have called
upon Admiral Schley to explain why he should publish a
letter giving an impression that no such colloquy had
occurred and refrain from publishing an accompanying
letter, and also a letter even previous to that, both of

which show that while this colloquy had not occurred in the exact terms alleged, it had substantially occurred; and why he offers no explanation of apparently permitting two letters containing the whole case to be withheld and another calculated to convey a different impression to be published. Certainly the action of the department in not so calling upon the admiral cannot be regarded as persecution.

The foregoing is all the action of the department in the matter of Admiral Schley, except that he has been detailed to the usual work given to officers of his and of higher rank in the ordinary discharge of naval duties, and has been accorded every facility for meeting the public.

There has undoubtedly been a great deal of discussion entirely outside of the department, which has itself, however, as yet expressed no opinion with regard to the maneuvers of our naval vessels at the battle of Santiago.

Nothing, therefore, could be further from the truth than the suggestion of persecution. Whatever has been done has been done with your approval and with a desire rather to allay than to stimulate the feeling which always attends a public discussion of personal merits. Admiral Schley neither has grounds for complaint nor has he suggested any complaint. Should he do so, the department would most cordially make any investigations he should desire, or submit to proper inquiry his record and his claims.

It is inconceivable that any self-respecting naval officer would for a moment rest under the criticism, much less the persecution, of a superior authority and not demand at once the hearing of a court of inquiry. Admiral Schley is an officer of long professional experience and has had every consideration at the hands of this department, and the fact that he has accepted its action without the sug-

II

gestion of an objection thereto is conclusive evidence that it has been entirely satisfactory to him or, if not, that it has been so just and considerate that he has no cause of complaint.

It may be that the Navy Department has made mistakes in this case, but if so, it certainly has not been in the direction of persecution.

Very respectfully,

(Signed)   JOHN D. LONG.

To the PRESIDENT.

B

PRESIDENT ROOSEVELT'S MEMORANDUM UPON THE
APPEAL OF ADMIRAL SCHLEY.

WHITE HOUSE,
February 18, 1902.

I HAVE received the appeal of Admiral Schley and the answer thereto from the Navy Department. I have examined both with the utmost care, as well as the preceding
appeal to the Secretary of the Navy. I have read through
all the testimony taken before the court and the statements of the counsel for Admirals Sampson and Schley;
have examined all the official reports of every kind in reference to the Santiago naval campaign, copies of the log-
books and signal-books, and the testimony before the
Court of Claims, and have also personally had before me
the four surviving captains of the five ships, aside from
those of the two admirals, which were actively engaged at
Santiago.

It appears that the Court of Inquiry was unanimous in
its findings of fact and unanimous in its expressions of
opinion on most of its findings of fact. No appeal is made
to me from the verdict of the court on these points where
it was unanimous. I have, however, gone carefully
over the evidence on these points also. I am satisfied
that on the whole the court did substantial justice. It
should have specifically condemned the failure to enforce
an efficient night blockade at Santiago while Admiral
Schley was in command. On the other hand, I feel that
there is a reasonable doubt whether he did not move his

squadron with sufficient expedition from port to port. The court is a unit in condemning Admiral Schley's action on the point where it seems to me he most gravely erred; his "retrograde movement" when he abandoned the blockade, and his disobedience of orders and misstatement of facts in relation thereto. It should be remembered, however, that the majority of these actions which the court censures occurred five weeks or more before the fight itself; and it certainly seems that if Admiral Schley's actions were censurable he should not have been left as second in command under Admiral Sampson. His offenses were in effect condoned when he was not called to account for them. Admiral Sampson, after the fight, in an official letter to the department alluded for the first time to Admiral Schley's "reprehensible conduct" six weeks previously. If Admiral Schley was guilty of reprehensible conduct of a kind which called for such notice from Admiral Sampson, then Admiral Sampson ought not to have left him as senior officer of the blockading squadron on the 3d of July, when he (Sampson) steamed away on his proper errand of communication with General Shafter.

We can therefore for our present purposes dismiss consideration of so much of the appeal as relates to anything except the battle. As regards this, the point raised in the appeal is between Admiral Sampson and Admiral Schley, as to which was in command, and as to which was entitled to the credit, if either of them was really entitled to any unusual and preëminent credit by any special exhibition of genius, skill, and courage. The court could have considered both of these questions, but as a matter of fact it unanimously excluded evidence offered upon them, and through its president announced its refusal to hear Admiral Sampson's side at all; and in view of such exclusion the majority of the court acted with entire propriety in not expressing any opinion on these points.   The matter has, however, been raised by the president of the court. Moreover, it is the point upon which Admiral Schley in his appeal lays most stress, and which he especially asks me to consider. I have therefore carefully investigated this matter also, and have informed myself upon it from the best sources of information at my command.

The appeal of Admiral Schley to me is not, as to this, the chief point he raises, really an appeal from the decision of the Court of Inquiry.   Five sixths of the appeal is devoted to this question of command and credit; that is, to matter which the Court of Inquiry did not consider.   It is in effect an appeal from the action of President McKinley three years ago when he sent in the recommendations for promotion for the various officers connected with the Santiago squadron, basing these recommendations upon his estimate of the credit to which the officers were respectively entitled.   What I have to decide, therefore, is whether or not President McKinley did injustice in the matter. This necessarily involves a comparison of the actions of the different commanders engaged. The exhaustive official reports of the action leave little to be brought out anew; but as the question of Admiral Sampson's right to be considered in chief command, which was determined in his favor by President McKinley, and later by the Court of Claims, has never hitherto been officially raised, I deemed it best to secure statements of the commanders of the five ships (other than the Brooklyn and New York, the flag-ships of the two admirals) which were actively engaged in the fight.

Admiral Philip is dead.   I quote extracts from his magazine article on the fight, written immediately after it occurred; closing with an extract from his letter to the Secretary of the Navy of February 27, 1899: —

"It was the blockade that made the battle possible. The battle was a direct consequence of the blockade, and upon the method and effectiveness of the blockade was very largely dependent the issue of the battle. . . . Under the orders of Admiral Sampson the blockade was conducted with a success exemplified by the result. . . . When the Spanish admiral at last made his dash to escape, we were ready — ready with our men, with our guns, and with our engines. . . . It was only a few minutes after we had seen the leader of the advancing squadron that it became apparent that Cervera's plan was to run his ships in column westward in an effort to escape. . . . Before he had fairly found himself outside the Morro the entire blockading squadron — Indiana, Oregon, Iowa, Brooklyn, and Texas — was pumping shell into him at such a rate as virtually to decide the issue of the battle in the first few moments. All our ships had closed in simultaneously. . . . Then occurred the incident which caused me for a moment more alarm than anything Cervera did that day. . . . Suddenly a whiff of breeze and a lull in the firing lifted the pall, and there bearing toward us and across our bows, turning on her port helm, with big waves curling over her bows and great clouds of black smoke pouring from her funnels, was the Brooklyn. She looked as big as half a dozen Great Easterns, and seemed so near that it took our breath away. 'Back both engines hard!' went down the tube to the astonished engineers, and in a twinkling the old ship was racing against herself. The collision which seemed imminent, even if it was not, was averted, and as the big cruiser glided past, all of us on the bridge gave a sigh of relief. Had the Brooklyn struck us then, it would probably have been the end of the Texas and her half thousand men. . . . At ten minutes to 10 (the Spanish ships had appeared at about 9.30) . . . the Iowa, Oregon,

and Texas were pretty well bunched, holding a parallel
course westward with the Spaniards. The Indiana was also
coming up, well inside of all the others of our squadron,
but a little in the rear, owing to her far eastward position
at starting. . . . About a quarter past 10 the Teresa, which
had been in difficulties from the moment she left the shelter of the Morro, turned to seek a beaching-place. She was
on fire, and we knew that she was no longer a quantity to
be reckoned with. Five minutes later our special enemy,
the Oquendo, also turned inshore. . . . The Vizcaya kept
blazing away viciously, but the pounding she got from our
four ships, more particularly the Oregon, was too much for
her, and in half an hour she too headed for the beach. . . .
I determined to push on with the Texas. . . . It gives me
pleasure to be able to write that, old ship as she is and not
built for speed, the Texas held her own and even gained
on the Colon in that chase. . . . Admiral Sampson was
commander-in-chief before, during, and after the action."

Captain Clark's statement is as follows : —

"The credit for the blockade which led up to the fight
is of course Admiral Sampson's. The position of the ships
on the morning of the fight in a semicircle head-on to the
harbor, in consequence of which we were able to close in
at once, was his. In closing in, that is, in making the first
movements, we were obeying his instructions ; though as
a matter of fact we would all have closed in any way,
instructions or no instructions. When the Spanish ships
came out of the harbor the navigator of my ship saw the
New York to the eastward, but I received no signal of any
kind from the New York during the action, nor was she
near enough to signal directly to me until after the Colon
surrendered.

"The engagement may be said to have been divided into
three parts : First, the fight proper, while the Spanish

squadron was coming out of the harbor and until it was
clear of the Diamond Shoals and definitely headed westward; second, the running fight with the already damaged
vessels as they fled westward, until the Teresa, Oquendo,
and Vizcaya ran ashore; and third, the chase of the Colon,
during which there was practically no fighting. During
the first stage I did not see the Brooklyn or receive any
signals from her. At the close of this stage the Oregon had
passed the Iowa and Texas, and when we burst out of
the smoke I saw the four Spanish ships going west apparently uninjured, and followed hard after, at the same time
observing the Brooklyn a little ahead and offshore. She
was broadside to the Spanish vessels and was receiving the
weight of their fire, and was returning it. The Brooklyn
and the Oregon thereafter occupied substantially these positions as regards each other, being about equidistant from
the Spanish ships as we successively overtook them, except when the Oregon attempted to close with the Oquendo.
The heaviest fighting was at the harbor mouth and while
the enemy was breaking through or passing our line. Not
long after the running fight began the Teresa and then
the Oquendo turned and went ashore, the Vizcaya continuing for some distance farther before she also was
beached. Throughout this running fight the Brooklyn
and Oregon were both hotly engaged, being ahead of any
of our other ships; and we then constituted the western
and what I regard as the then fighting division of our fleet.
I considered Commodore Schley in responsible command
during this running fight and chase so far as I was concerned, and acknowledged and repeated a signal he had
flying, for close action or something of the kind. As, however, the problem was perfectly simple, namely, to pursue
the Spanish ships as I had been doing before I saw the
Brooklyn, he did not as a matter of fact exercise any con-

trol over any movement or action of the Oregon, nor did I perform any action of any kind whatever in obedience to any order from the Brooklyn, neither as to my course nor as to my speed, nor as to my gun-fire, during the fight or chase.

"The Oregon always had fires under all boilers. In spite of the speed shown by the Oregon in this fight, she had not been and is not classed as the fastest ship; but during all her service, in order that no scale should form in them, not one of our boilers was used for condensing, though the resulting discomfort for all hands was an additional hardship for her commanding officer."

The following is Admiral Evans's statement : —

"The credit for the blockade, for the arrangement of the ships at the opening of the fight, and for the first movements forward into the fight must of course belong to Admiral Sampson, whose orders we were putting into effect. When the fight began Admiral Sampson's ship, the New York, was in plain sight. I saw her turning to overtake us. Throughout the fight I considered myself as under his command, but I received no orders from him until the Vizcaya was aground. Nor did I receive any orders whatever from the Brooklyn, nor should I have heeded them if I had received them, inasmuch as I considered Admiral Sampson to be present and in command.

"The heavy fighting was during the time when the Spanish vessels were coming out of the harbor and before they had stretched fairly to the westward. When they thus stretched to the westward we all went after them without orders — of course we could do nothing else. Until the Teresa and Oquendo ran ashore the Iowa was close behind the Oregon and ahead of the Texas, and all of us were firing steadily at the Spanish ships. The Texas then recovered her speed — for she was dead in

the water after having backed to avoid the Brooklyn
when the Brooklyn turned — and she went ahead of the
Iowa. Both of us continued to fire at the Vizcaya until
she went ashore. Then I stopped, but the Texas followed
the Brooklyn and the Oregon after the Colon.

"When the battle began, the New York was not much
farther to the eastward of me than the Brooklyn was to
the westward. After the Vizcaya had grounded the New
York overtook me and signaled me to return to the
mouth of the harbor to prevent any other Spanish ship
from coming out and attacking the transports. I received
no signals of any kind from the Brooklyn. All we had
to do was to close in on the Spanish squadron as it came
out of the harbor, in obedience to the orders of Admiral
Sampson, and then, when the heaviest fighting was over
and the Spanish ships were trying to escape to the west,
to follow them — and of course there was no signal necessary to tell us to follow a fleeing enemy.

"The machinery of the Iowa was not in condition to
get the best speed, though every effort had been made
to make it so. Her cylinder-heads had not been off for
more than six months, owing to the service she was per-
forming. Her bottom was very foul, as she had not been
docked for a period of seventeen months. The Indiana
was unavoidably in even worse shape.

"The New York had left the blockading line flying the
signal 'Disregard the movements of the commander-in-
chief,' a signal frequently made, and well understood by
the entire fleet. It did not transfer the command. No
signal was made for the second in command to assume
command of the fleet, which was usually done by the
commander-in-chief before reaching the limit of signal
distance when he proposed for any reason temporarily to
relinquish his command to the next ranking officer."

The following is Admiral Taylor's statement: —

"At the beginning of the fight the New York was about as far to the eastward of me as the Brooklyn was to the westward. The only signal I received from the New York was at the very close of the fight, when she signaled to me to return and guard the mouth of the harbor so that nothing should come out to attack our transports. I received no signal whatever from the Brooklyn, and should not have heeded any if one had been made, as I considered Admiral Sampson present and in command. From her position the Indiana took full part in the actual fight as the Spanish ships came out of the harbor. When they ran to the westward the Indiana fell behind, but continued firing at them and at the torpedo-boats until all but the Colon were sunk or beached. I saw the Brooklyn turn and run out seaward, seemingly over a mile, about the time the rear one of the Spanish ships turned to the west; if instead of making this loop the Brooklyn had stood straight in towards the Spaniards, as the other American ships did, it seemed to me that the fight would have been settled then, without need of the long chase."

The following is Commander Wainwright's statement:

"At the outset of the fight the New York was not much farther away from me in one direction than the Brooklyn was in the other and was in plain sight. A signal from Admiral Taylor in connection with my moving forward to attack the torpedo-boats was the only signal I received. I made one to the New York just before the last torpedo-boat sank. The New York at that time was coming up under the fire of the batteries, and herself fired a couple of shots at the torpedo-boat. Of course Admiral Sampson was present and in command. I received no signals from the Brooklyn, and would not

have noticed her at all had it not been for the fact that
when the other vessels closed in she made what has been
since called 'the loop,' so that my attention was attracted
by not seeing the Texas because she stopped, and by not
seeing the Brooklyn because she went to seaward, away
from the Spanish vessels. In other words, the left or
westward part of our line was refused, and this attracted
my attention, because it seemed to me from where I was
that this permitted the Spanish vessels to try to escape
to westward."

The survey of the damages of the four Spanish war-
vessels shows that in addition to several score hits by
the 6-pounder and 1-pounder guns of the American fleet,
they were struck forty-three times by the larger guns of
four inches caliber and over. The Colon, which came out
inside the others and did comparatively little fighting,
received but three of these hits. The other three ships,
which bore the brunt of the action, received forty among
them. Of these forty, eleven, according to the report of
the board which examined into them, were by 4-inch guns,
ten by 5-inch guns, four by either 4 or 5 inch (the board
could not determine which), while one was by either a
5 or 6 inch, twelve were by 8-inch, and two by 12-inch
guns. All of our big ships except the Texas had 8-inch
guns. Only the Texas and Iowa had 12-inch guns. The
Oregon and Indiana had 13-inch guns; and they and the
Texas had 6-inch guns. The only 4-inch guns were on
the Iowa; the only 5-inch guns on the Brooklyn. Therefore on the three Spanish ships which did the bulk of the
fighting, out of the forty large-caliber shots that struck
them eleven certainly came from the Iowa, ten certainly
came from the Brooklyn, four from either the Iowa or
the Brooklyn, and two from either the Iowa or the Texas.

Of the three which struck the Colon two were 5-inch and must have come from the Brooklyn; one was either a 5-inch or a 6-inch. It must be remembered that the 4 and 5 inch guns were the only quick-firers above 6-pounders in our fleet, and that they were not only much more rapidly but much more surely handled than were the larger and slower-firing guns. The damage and loss of the American vessels were trivial. The only loss suffered was aboard the Brooklyn, where one man was killed and one wounded. In damage, the cost of the repairs shows that the Iowa suffered most and the Oregon least. The American ships engaged possessed a more than twofold material superiority over the Spanish ships, and the difference in the handling of their guns and their engines was even greater. We have just cause to be proud of the vigilance and instant readiness our ships displayed, and the workmanlike efficiency with which they were handled. The most striking act was that of the Gloucester, a converted yacht, which her commander, Wainwright, pushed into the fight through a hail of projectiles, any one of which would have sunk her, in order that he might do his part in destroying the two torpedo-boats, each possessing far more than his own offensive power.

From the statements of the captains above, from the official reports, and from the testimony before the Court of Inquiry, the fight can be plotted with absolute certainty in its important outlines, though there is conflict as to minor points. When the four Spanish cruisers came out of the harbor the New York had left her position in the blockading line forty or forty-five minutes before. She had hoisted the signal "Disregard the movements of the commander-in-chief," but had not hoisted the signal to the second in command to take charge, which, as appears

by the signal-book, was sometimes but not always used
when the command was transferred. As soon as the
engagement began the New York turned and steamed
back, hoisting a signal to close in, which, however, none
of the squadron saw. She was in plain sight, and not
very much farther from the easternmost blockading ships
than the latter were from the Brooklyn, which was the
westernmost of the line. As soon as the Spanish ships
appeared the five big American blockaders started toward
them in accordance with the standing orders of Admiral
Sampson. After this first move each acted purely on his
own initiative. For some minutes the Spanish and American vessels steadily approached one another, and the
fighting was at its hottest. Then the already damaged
Spanish ships turned to the westward, while at the same
time the westernmost American vessel, the Brooklyn,
which was nearest the Spanish line, turned to the eastward, making a loop or three-quarter circle, at the end of
which she again headed westward, farther off from and
farther behind the Spanish vessels than before the loop
had begun, but still ahead of any of the American vessels,
although farther outside. The Texas, the next ship to
the Brooklyn, either was or conceived herself to be put
in such jeopardy by the Brooklyn's turn toward her that
she backed her engines, coming almost or quite to a
standstill; so that both the Oregon and the Iowa, which
were originally to the eastward of her, passed her, and it
was some time after she again started before she regained
her former position relatively to the Spanish vessels.
The Spanish vessels had straightened out in column for
the west, the Colon going inside of the others and gradually forging ahead of them, without suffering much
damage. The two torpedo-boats, which had followed
them out of the harbor, were now destroyed by the fire

of the rearmost of the American big vessels and of the Gloucester, which headed straight in for them, paying no more heed to their quick-fire guns than to the heavy artillery of the forts, to which she was also exposed.

In the running fight which followed, until the Teresa, Oquendo, and Vizcaya were destroyed, the Indiana gradually dropped behind, although she continued to fire until the last of the three vessels went ashore. The Brooklyn was ahead of any of the other American vessels on a course outside theirs ; she was nearly broadside on to the Spaniards. The Oregon, Iowa, and Texas were all close together and actively engaged throughout this running fight. The Brooklyn and Oregon, followed at some distance by the Texas, then continued in chase of the Colon, which went nearly thirty miles farther before she also went ashore. During this chase of the Colon there was practically no fighting.

These are the facts as set forth above in the statements of the captains, and elsewhere in their official reports and testimony. They leave no room for doubt on any important point.

The question of command is in this case nominal and technical. Admiral Sampson's ship, the New York, was seen at the outset of the fight from all the other ships except the Brooklyn. Four of these five ship captains have testified that they regarded him as present and in command. He signaled " Close in " to the fleet as soon as the first Spanish ship appeared, but his signal was not seen by any American vessel. He was actually under fire from the forts, and himself fired a couple of shots, at the close of the action with the torpedo-boats, in addition to signaling the Indiana just at the close of the action. But during the action not a single order from him was received by any of the ships that were actively engaged.

Admiral Schley at the outset of the action hoisted the two signals of "Clear ship" and "Close in," which was simply carrying out the standing orders of Admiral Sampson as to what should be done if the enemy's ships attempted to break out of the harbor. Until after the close of the first portion of the fight at the mouth of the harbor, and until after he had made his loop and the Spanish ships were fleeing to the westward, not another American ship noticed a signal from him. When the western pursuit had begun the Oregon, and the Oregon only, noticed and repeated one of his signals of command. The captain of the Oregon then regarded him as in command, but did not in any shape or way execute any movement or any action of any kind whatsoever in accordance with any order from him.

In short, the question as to which of the two men, Admiral Sampson or Admiral Schley, was at the time in command, is of merely nominal character. Technically Sampson commanded the fleet, and Schley, as usual, the western division. The actual fact, the important fact, is that after the battle was joined not a helm was shifted, not a gun was fired, not a pound of steam was put on in the engine-room aboard any ship actively engaged, in obedience to the order of either Sampson or Schley, save on their own two vessels. It was a captains' fight.

Therefore the credit to which each of the two is entitled rests on matters apart from the claim of nominal command over the squadron; for so far as the actual fight was concerned neither one nor the other in fact exercised any command. Sampson was hardly more than technically in the fight. His real claim for credit rests upon his work as commander-in-chief; upon the excellence of the blockade; upon the preparedness of the squadron; upon the arrangement of the ships head-on in a semicircle around the harbor; and the standing orders in accordance with which they instantly moved to the attack of the Spaniards when the latter appeared. For all these things the credit is his.

Admiral Schley is rightly entitled — as is Captain Cook — to the credit of what the Brooklyn did in the fight. On the whole she did well; but I agree with the unanimous finding of the three admirals who composed the Court of Inquiry as to the "loop." It seriously marred the Brooklyn's otherwise excellent record, being in fact the one grave mistake made by any American ship that day. Had the Brooklyn turned to the westward, that is, in the same direction that the Spanish ships were going, instead of in the contrary direction, she would undoubtedly have been in more "dangerous proximity" to them. But it would have been more dangerous for them as well as for her! This kind of danger must not be too nicely weighed by those whose trade it is to dare greatly for the honor of the flag. Moreover, the danger was certainly not as great as that which, in the self-same moment, menaced Wainwright's fragile craft as he drove forward against the foe. It was not in my judgment as great as the danger to which the Texas was exposed by the turn as actually made. It certainly caused both the Brooklyn and the Texas materially to lose position compared to the fleeing Spanish vessels. But after the loop had once been taken Admiral Schley handled the Brooklyn manfully and well. She and the Oregon were thenceforth the headmost of the American vessels — though the Iowa certainly, and seemingly the Texas also, did as much in hammering to a standstill the Vizcaya, Oquendo, and Teresa; while the Indiana did all her eastward position and crippled machinery permitted. In the chase of the Colon the Brooklyn and Oregon share the credit between them.

II

Under such circumstances it seems to me that the recommendations of President McKinley were eminently proper, and that so far as Admirals Sampson and Schley were concerned it would have been unjust for him to have made other recommendations. Personally I feel that in view of Captain Clark's long voyage in the Oregon and the condition in which he brought her to the scene of service, as well as the way in which he actually managed her before and during the fight, it would have been well to have given him the same advancement that was given Wainwright. But waiving this, it is evident that Wainwright was entitled to receive more than any of the other commanders; and that it was just to Admiral Sampson that he should receive a greater advance in numbers than Admiral Schley — there was nothing done in the battle that warranted any unusual reward for either. In short, as regards Admirals Sampson and Schley, I find that President McKinley did substantial justice, and that there would be no warrant for reversing his action.

Both Admiral Sampson and Admiral Schley are now on the retired list. In concluding their report the members of the Court of Inquiry, Admirals Dewey, Benham, and Ramsay, unite in stating that they recommend that no further action be had in the matter. With this recommendation I most heartily concur. There is no excuse whatever from either side for any further agitation of this unhappy controversy. To keep it alive would merely do damage to the navy and to the country.

THEODORE ROOSEVELT.

C

SPEECH OF THE HON. JOHN D. LONG, SECRETARY OF
THE NAVY, ON THE OCCASION OF THE PRESENTA-
TION OF THE SWORD — THE NATION'S GIFT — TO
ADMIRAL DEWEY ON OCTOBER 3, 1899.

MY DEAR ADMIRAL, — Let me read a few extracts from
our official correspondence, covering less than a fortnight's
time, and now known the world over : —

WASHINGTON, APRIL 24, 1898.

DEWEY, HONGKONG.

War has commenced between the United States and Spain.
Proceed at once to Philippine Islands. Begin operations at once,
particularly against the Spanish fleet. You must capture vessels
or destroy. Use utmost endeavors.

LONG.

MANILA, May 1.

SECRETARY OF THE NAVY, WASHINGTON.

The squadron arrived at Manila at daybreak this morning.
Immediately engaged enemy and destroyed the following vessels.
. . . The squadron is uninjured. Few men were slightly wounded.

DEWEY.

May 4.

SECRETARY OF THE NAVY, WASHINGTON.

I have taken possession of the naval station, Philippine Islands.
I control bay completely and can take city at any time. The
squadron excellent health and spirits. I am assisting and protecting Spanish sick and wounded.

DEWEY.

WASHINGTON, May 7, 1898.

DEWEY.

The President, in the name of the American people, thanks you
and your officers and men for your splendid achievement and over-

whelming victory. In recognition, he has appointed you acting rear-admiral, and will recommend a vote of thanks to you by Congress as a foundation for further promotion.

LONG.

In these few words what a volume of history; what a record of swift, high, heroic discharge of duty! You went; you saw; you conquered. It seems but yesterday that the Republic, full of anxiety, strained its listening ear to catch the first word from those distant islands of the sea. It came flashing over the wires that May morning as the sun bursts through the clouds, and filled every heart with the illumination of its good cheer. In the twinkling of an eye your name was on every lip; the blessing of every American was on your head; and your country strode instantly forward, a mightier power among the nations of the world. As we welcome you back, there comes back also the vivid picture of that time, with all its hopes and fears, and then with all its swift succeeding triumph and glory.

Let me now read the act of Congress in pursuance of which we are here: —

Resolved, by the Senate and the House of Representatives of the United States of America in Congress assembled, That the Secretary of the Navy be, and he hereby is, authorized to present a sword of honor to Commodore George Dewey, and to cause to be struck bronze medals, commemorating the battle of Manila Bay, and to distribute such medals to the officers and men of the ships of the Asiatic Squadron of the United States under command of Commodore George Dewey on May 1, 1898, and that, to enable the Secretary to carry out this resolution, the sum of $10,000.00, or so much thereof as may be necessary, is hereby appropriated out of any money in the Treasury not otherwise appropriated.

Approved June 3, 1898.

It was by this solemn enactment, approved by the President, that the people of the United States made provision for putting in material form one expression of their appreciation of your valor as an officer of their navy, and of your great achievement as their representative in opening the door to a new era in the civilization of the world. The victory of Manila Bay gave you rank with the most distinguished naval heroes of all time. Nor was your merit most in the brilliant victory which you achieved in a battle fought with the utmost gallantry and skill, waged without error, and crowned with overwhelming success. It was still more in the nerve with which you sailed from Hongkong to Manila Harbor; in the spirit of your conception of attack; in your high commanding confidence as a leader who had weighed every risk and prepared for every emergency, and who also had the unfaltering determination to win and that utter freedom from the thought of possibility of swerving from his purpose which are the very assurance of victory. No captain ever faced a more crucial test than when that morning, bearing the fate and the honor of your country in your hand, thousands of miles from home, with every foreign port in the world shut to you, nothing between you and annihilation but the thin sheathing of your ships, your cannon, and your devoted officers and men, you moved upon the enemy's batteries on shore and on sea with unflinching faith and nerve, and before the sun was halfway up the heavens had silenced the guns of the foe, sunk the hostile fleet, demonstrated the supremacy of American sea power, and transferred to the United States an imperial cluster of the Islands of the Pacific. Later, by your display of large powers of administration, by your poise and prudence, and by your great discretion, not only in act but also in word, which is almost more important, you proved yourself a great representative citizen of the United States, as

well as already its great naval hero. The luster of the
American Navy was gloriously bright before, and you
have added to it a new luster. Its constellation of stars
was glorious before, and you have added to it another
star of the first magnitude. And yet many of your grateful countrymen feel that, in the time to come, it may be
your still greater honor that you struck the first blow,
under the providence of God, in the enfranchisement of
those beautiful islands which make that great empire of
the sea, in relieving them from the bondage and oppression of centuries, and in putting them on their way, under
the protecting shield of your country's guidance, to take
their place in the civilization, the arts, the industries, the
liberties, and all the good things of the most enlightened
and happy nations of the world, so that generations hence
your name shall be to them a household word, enshrined
in their history and in their hearts. Clouds and darkness
may linger about them now, but the shining outcome is
as sure as the rising of the sun. Whatever the passing
tribulations and difficulties of the present moment, they
will in due time soon and surely give way to the dawn of
a glorious new day — a day not of any mere selfish imperial dominion of one people over another, but of the
imperial moral and physical growth and expansion of all
the people, whatever their race or language or color, who
have come under the shelter of the broad shield of the
United States of America.

By authorizing the presentation of this sword to you
as the mark of its approval your country has recognized,
therefore, not only the rich fruits which, even before
returning from your victory, you have poured into her
lap, but also her own responsibility to discharge the great
trust which is thus put upon her and fulfill the destiny of
her own growth and of the empire that is now her charge.

It is a new demand upon all the resources of her conscience, wisdom, and courage. It is a work in the speedy beneficent consummation of which she is entitled to the cordial help, sympathy, and uplift of all her citizens — not the faint-hearted doubts and teasing cavils of any of them. It is a work on which she has entered in the interest of early peace in these new lands, their stable government, the establishment in them of law and order, and the security of life and property and the American standards of prosperity and home. Let those who fear remember that though her children, guided by you, take the wings of the morning and dwell in the uttermost parts of the sea, even there the hand of our fathers' God shall lead them and His right hand shall hold them. In this work, in view of the great part you have taken in the sudden development of her sovereignty, your full knowledge of the situation, and the just hold you have on the hearts of all her people, she looks for your continued service and listens for your counsel in the high hope and purpose that the triumph of her peace shall be even greater than her triumph in war.

It is my good fortune, under the terms of the enactment of Congress, to have the honor of presenting to you this beautiful sword. If during the many coming years which I trust will be yours of useful service to your country it shall remain sheathed in peace, as God grant it may, that fact will perhaps be due more than to anything else to the thoroughness with which you have already done its work. I congratulate you on your return across the sea in full health of mind and body to receive it here; here in the national capital; here on these consecrated steps where Lincoln stood; here, standing between the statue of the first President of the United States and him who is its living President to-day; here in this beautiful city adorned with the statues of its statesmen and heroes, the number incomplete until your own is added; here among this throng of citizens, who are only a type of the millions and millions more who are all animated by the same spirit of affectionate and grateful welcome. I cannot doubt that it is one of the proudest days of your life, and I know that it is one of the happiest in the heart of each one of your fellow countrymen, wherever they are, whether on the continent, or on the far-off islands of the sea.

Now, following the authorization of Congress, I present this sword of honor which I hold in my hand — my hand! — rather let it go to you through the hand of one who in his youth also periled his life and fought for his country in battle, and who to-day is the commander-in-chief of all our armies and navies, the President of the United States.

D

PROMOTIONS FOR EMINENT AND CONSPICUOUS CONDUCT IN BATTLE, OR FOR EXTRAORDINARY HEROISM DURING THE WAR BETWEEN THE UNITED STATES AND SPAIN.

For eminent and conspicuous conduct at the battle of Manila Bay, May 1, 1898.

NAME.	RANK AT TIME OF SERVICE.	PROMOTION.
George Dewey,	Commodore,	To Rear-Admiral. To Admiral by act of Congress, Mar. 2, 1899.
Frank Wildes,	Captain,	5 numbers.
Joseph B. Coghlan,	Captain,	6 numbers.
Charles V. Gridley,	Captain,	6 numbers.
Nehemiah M. Dyer,	Captain,	7 numbers.
Benjamin P. Lamberton,	Captain,	7 numbers.
Asa Walker,	Commander,	9 numbers.
Edward P. Wood,	Commander,	10 numbers.
John D. Ford,	Chief Engineer,	3 numbers.
Richard Inch,	Chief Engineer,	3 numbers.
Frederic Singer,	Lieutenant,	5 numbers.
John B. Briggs,	Lieutenant-Commander,	5 numbers.
George P. Colvocoresses,	Lieutenant-Commander,	5 numbers.
John A. Norris,	Lieutenant-Commander,	5 numbers.
Edward M. Hughes,	Lieutenant,	5 numbers.
Corwin P. Rees,	Lieutenant,	5 numbers.
George B. Ransom,	Chief Engineer,	3 numbers.
Frank H. Bailey,	Chief Engineer,	3 numbers.
Benjamin Tappan,	Lieutenant,	5 numbers.
Reynold T. Hall,	Passed Assistant Engineer,	3 numbers.
Thomas M. Brumby,	Lieutenant,	5 numbers.
Harry H. Caldwell,	Ensign,	5 numbers.
William P. Scott,	Ensign,	5 numbers.
William R. White,	Naval Cadet,	5 numbers.
James Entwistle,	Chief Engineer,	2 numbers.

For eminent and conspicuous conduct at the battle of Santiago,
July 3, 1898.

NAME.	RANK AT TIME OF SERVICE.	PROMOTION.
Francis J. Higginson,	Captain,	3 numbers.
Robley D. Evans,	Captain,	5 numbers.
Henry C. Taylor,	Captain,	5 numbers.
Francis A. Cook,	Captain,	5 numbers.
Charles E. Clark,	Captain,	6 numbers.[1]
French E. Chadwick,	Captain,	5 numbers.
Alexander B. Bates,	Chief Engineer,	3 numbers.
Robert W. Milligan,	Chief Engineer,	3 numbers.
Charles W. Rae,	Chief Engineer,	3 numbers.
Raymond P. Rodgers,	Lieutenant-Commander,	5 numbers.
Seaton Schroeder,	Lieutenant-Commander,	3 numbers.
Richard Wainwright,	Lieutenant-Commander,	10 numbers.
John A. Rodgers,	Lieutenant-Commander,	5 numbers.
James K. Cogswell,	Lieutenant-Commander,	5 numbers.
William P. Potter,	Lieutenant-Commander,	5 numbers.
Giles B. Harber,	Lieutenant-Commander,	5 numbers.
Newton E. Mason,	Lieutenant-Commander,	5 numbers.
Warner B. Bayley,	Chief Engineer,	2 numbers.
Alexander Sharp, Jr.,	Lieutenant,	5 numbers.
George W. McElroy,	Passed Assistant Engineer,	3 numbers.
Harry McL. P. Huse,	Lieutenant,	5 numbers.
Cleland N. Offley,	Passed Assistant Engineer,	4 numbers.
Joseph M. Reeves,	Assistant Engineer,	4 numbers.
Frank Lyon,	Assistant Engineer,	4 numbers.
Charles J. McConnell,	Chief Engineer,	1 number.
John L. Hannum,	Chief Engineer,	2 numbers.
George Cowie,	Chief Engineer,	3 numbers.

[1] Received a further advancement of 7 numbers June 18, 1902.

APPENDIX 219

FOR EMINENT AND CONSPICUOUS CONDUCT ON OCCASIONS MENTIONED.

Name.	Rank at Time of Service.	Promotion.	Service for which Rewarded.
John J. Hunker,	Commander,	3 numbers,	Proceeding July 21, 1898, with Annapolis under his command, over a mine field at Nipe Bay to attack inside.
Chapman C. Todd,	Commander,	3 numbers,	Engagements at Cardenas May 12, and Manzanillo July 18, 1898.
William T. Swinburne,	Commander,	2 numbers,	Attacks on batteries of Tunas July 1, 3, and 26, 1898.
Adolph Marix,	Lieutenant-Commander,	2 numbers,	Engagements at Manzanillo July 1 and 18, 1898.
Albert C. Dillingham,	Lieutenant-Commander,	2 numbers,	Battle off Cienfuegos May 11, 1898.
Aaron Ward,	Lieutenant,	2 numbers,	Engagement with Spanish gunboat Don Gorge Juan July 21, 1898.
Lucien Young,	Lieutenant,	3 numbers,	Engagements at Manzanillo June 30, July 18, and Aug. 12, 1898.
James M. Helm,	Lieutenant,	5 numbers,	Engagement at Manzanillo June 30, 1898.
Carl W. Jungen,	Lieutenant,	5 numbers,	Engagement at Manzanillo June 30, 1898.
Charles H. Harlow,	Lieutenant,	2 numbers,	Extricating two steam launches from Spanish ambuscade near Santiago June 17, 1898.

FOR EMINENT AND CONSPICUOUS CONDUCT ON OCCASIONS MENTIONED —
(Continued).

NAME.	RANK AT TIME OF SERVICE.	PROMOTION.	SERVICE FOR WHICH REWARDED.
John B. Bernadou,	Lieutenant,	10 numbers,	Engagement at Cardenas May 11, 1898.
John L. Purcell,	Lieutenant,	2 numbers,	Engagements at Manzanillo and Tunas.
Thomas P. Magruder,	Ensign,	5 numbers,	Pulling off launches under heavy Spanish fire May 11, 1898.
Walter S. Crosley,	Ensign,	2 numbers,	Engagement with Spanish gunboat Don Gorge Juan July 21, 1898.
Andre M. Procter,	Assistant Engineer,	5 numbers,	Engagement between Gloucester and Spanish torpedo-boat destroyers July 3, 1898.
Frederick Muller,	Mate,	To Boatswain,	Engagement off Manzanillo June 30, 1898.
Thomas C. Wood,	Volunteer Lieutenant,	8 numbers,	Engagement between Gloucester and Spanish torpedo-boat destroyers July 3, 1898.
George H. Norman,	Volunteer Lieutenant,	8 numbers,	Engagement between Gloucester and Spanish torpedo-boat destroyers July 3, 1898.
John T. Edson,	Volunteer Lieutenant,	8 numbers,	Engagement between Gloucester and Spanish torpedo-boat destroyers July 3, 1898.

John F. Bransford,	Volunteer Assistant Surgeon,	3 numbers,	Engagement between Gloucester and Spanish torpedo-boat destroyers July 3, 1898.
Alexander Brown,	Volunteer Assistant Paymaster,	3 numbers,	Engagement between Gloucester and Spanish torpedo-boat destroyers July 3, 1898.

FOR EXTRAORDINARY HEROISM ON OCCASIONS MENTIONED.

NAME.	RANK AT TIME OF SERVICE.	PROMOTION.	SERVICE FOR WHICH REWARDED.
Charles D. Sigsbee,	Captain,	3 numbers,	As captain of the Maine, and in fight with Spanish torpedo-boat destroyer Terror, June 22, 1898.
Cameron McR. Winslow,	Lieutenant,	5 numbers,	Cable-cutting expedition off Cienfuegos May 11, 1898.
Edwin A. Anderson,	Lieutenant,	5 numbers,	Cable-cutting expedition off Cienfuegos May 11, 1898.
Victor Blue,	Lieutenant (junior grade),	5 numbers,	Perilous reconnoitering duty near Santiago, Cuba.
William H. Buck,	Ensign,	8 numbers,	Service in disguise in Spain.
Henry H. Ward,	Ensign,	10 numbers,	Service in disguise in Spain and Porto Rico.
James P. Morton,	Assistant Engineer,	4 numbers,	Entering at great personal peril fire-room of Vixen May 28, 1898, to repair boiler.

FOR EXTRAORDINARY HEROISM ON OCCASIONS MENTIONED.—*(Continued)*.

NAME.	RANK AT TIME OF SERVICE.	PROMOTION.	SERVICE FOR WHICH REWARDED.
Wm. W. Galt,	Paymaster,	1 number,	Perilous voyage from Hongkong to Mirs Bay in small steam launch April 26, 1898, to aid in expediting departure of American squadron for Manila Bay.
Richmond P. Hobson,	Naval Constructor with rank of Lieutenant,	10 numbers,	Sinking collier Merrimac in Santiago harbor June 3, 1898.
Joseph W. Powell,	Naval Cadet,	2 numbers,	Command of steam launch which accompanied collier Merrimac.

ADVANCED FOR EMINENT AND CONSPICUOUS CONDUCT IN BATTLE IN THE PHILIPPINES AND IN CHINA.

NAME.	RANK AT TIME OF SERVICE.	PROMOTION.	SERVICE FOR WHICH REWARDED.
Bowman H. McCalla,	Captain,	3 numbers,	In battles engaged in by Pekin relief column under Vice-Admiral Seymour.
Cleland Davis,	Lieutenant,	5 numbers,	In battles March 25, 27, and 28, and April 4, 1899, during operations with Second Division, Eighth Army Corps, Philippine Islands.

Emory Winship,	Ensign,	4 numbers,	Battle at Mallabon, Philippine Islands, March 4, 1899.
Daniel W. Wurtzbaugh,	Ensign,	4 numbers,	Battles June 20, 21, and 22, 1900, while with relief column under Vice-Admiral Seymour.
Charles E. Gilpin,	Ensign,	3 numbers,	Battles June 20, 21, and 22, 1900, while with relief column under Vice-Admiral Seymour.
Joseph K. Taussig,	Naval Cadet,	4 numbers,	Battles June 20, 21, and 22, 1900, while with relief column under Vice-Admiral Seymour.
Charles E. Courtney,	Naval Cadet,	6 numbers,	Battles June 20, 21, 22, and 27, 1900, while with relief column under Vice-Admiral Seymour.
Thomas M. Lippitt,	Assistant Surgeon,	2 numbers,	Defense of legations in Pekin July 3, 1900.
Henry E. Jewett,	Paymaster,	2 numbers,	Battles June 20, 21, and 22, 1900, while with relief column under Vice-Admiral Seymour.
Clifford H. Sheldon,	Gunner,	3 numbers,	Battles June 20, 21, and 22, 1900, while with relief column under Vice-Admiral Seymour.
John T. Myers,	Captain U. S. M. C.,	4 numbers,	Leading charge on Chinese barricade, Pekin, July 3, 1900.
Littleton W. T. Waller,	Major U. S. M. C.,	2 numbers,	Battles June 21 and 23, 1900, and July 3 and 9, 1900.
Smedley D. Butler,	First Lieutenant U. S. M. C.,	2 numbers,	Battle of Tientsin.
Henry Leonard,	First Lieutenant U. S. M. C.,	2 numbers,	Battle of Tientsin, July 13, 1900.

OFFICERS OF THE MARINE CORPS ADVANCED FOR DISTINGUISHED CONDUCT IN THE PRESENCE OF THE ENEMY.

NAME.	RANK AT TIME OF SERVICE.	PROMOTION.	SERVICE FOR WHICH REWARDED.
Littleton W. T. Waller,	Major U. S. M. C.,	Brevetted Lieutenant-Colonel,	Distinguished conduct in presence of enemy July 13, 1900.
John T. Myers, Smedley D. Butler,	Captain U. S. M. C., Captain U. S. M. C.,	Brevetted Major, Brevetted Captain,	Defense of legations in Pekin. In battle of Tientsin July 13, 1900.
Charles G. Andresen,	Captain U. S. M. C.,	Brevetted Captain,	In battle of Tientsin July 13, 1900.
Wade L. Jolly,	First Lieutenant U. S. M. C.,	Brevetted First Lieutenant,	Capture East Arsenal, Tientsin, June 27, 1900.
Arthur E. Harding, Geo. C. Thorpe,	First Lieutenant U. S. M. C., Captain U. S. M. C.,	Brevetted Captain, Brevetted Captain,	Battle Tientsin June 21, 1900. Engagement Novalita, Philippine Islands, Oct. 8, 1899.
David D. Porter,	Captain U. S. M. C.,	Brevetted Captain,	Engagement Novalita, Philippine Islands, Oct. 8, 1899.
Robert L. Meade,	Colonel U. S. M. C.,	Brevetted Brigadier-General,	In battle Tientsin July 13, 1900.
William G. Powell,	First Lieutenant U. S. M. C.,	Brevetted Captain,	In battle Tientsin, June 21, 1900.
George Richards,	Major U. S. M. C.,	Brevetted Lieutenant-Colonel,	In battle Tientsin, July 13, 1900.
Newt H. Hall,	Captain U. S. M. C.,	Brevetted Major,	Siege of Pekin, June 20 to Aug. 14, 1900.

E

FROM SAMPSON'S REPORT OF ATTACK ON PORTO RICO

U. S. Flagship New York,
Key West, Florida, May 18, 1898.

Sir :—

Supplementary to my telegram No. 73 of the 12th instant I have the honor to submit the following report more in detail, of the attack on the defenses of Porto Rico, made by a portion of this squadron on the 12th instant.

Upon approaching San Juan it was seen that none of the Spanish vessels were in the harbor. I was therefore considerably in doubt whether they had reached San Juan and again departed for some unknown destination, or whether they had not arrived. As their capture was the object of the expedition, and as it was essential that they should not pass to the westward, I determined to attack the batteries defending the port, in order to develop their position and strength, and then, without waiting to reduce the city or subject it to a regular bombardment, — which would require due notice, — turn to the westward.

Our progress had been so much slower than I had reason to anticipate, from Key West to Porto Rico, owing to the frequent break-downs of the two monitors, which made it necessary to tow them both the whole distance, and also to the disabled condition of the Indiana, that eight days had been consumed instead of five, as I had estimated.

I commenced the attack as soon as it was good daylight. This lasted about three hours, when the signal
was made to discontinue the firing, and the squadron
stood to the northeast until out of sight of San Juan,
when the course was laid for the westward, with the view
of communicating with the department at Porto Rico, and
learn if the department had obtained information as to
the movements of the Spanish vessels.

At Cape Haytien I received word from the department
that the Spanish vessels had been sighted off Curaçoa on
the 14th instant and directed me to return with all dispatch to Key West.

As stated in my telegram, no serious injury was done
any of the ships, and only one man was killed and seven
wounded slightly. . . .

.   .   .   .

Very respectfully,
W. T. SAMPSON,
Rear-Admiral U. S. Navy,
Commander-in-Chief U. S. Naval Forces,
North Atlantic Station.

THE SECRETARY OF THE NAVY,
NAVY DEPARTMENT, WASHINGTON, D. C.

INDEX

INDEX

The Riverside Press
Electrotyped and printed by H. O. Houghton & Co.
Cambridge, Mass., U. S. A.